Once in a great while, a [...] t
gives me insight, encoura [...] [...]
person God created me t [...] .
piece that should be revi [...] .1
that speaks to how God grows us and calls us through all seasons of life, from
childhood to senior years.

DAVE HATAJ | Author of *Good Work*; CEO of Edgerton Gear, Inc.

This book was a journey in self-reflection. It was a chance for finding where I am
along the path, where I might be headed, and how God has shaped the road on
which I find myself. Leadership is often about seeing the bigger picture. Self-lead-
ership, a skill we all need to practice, relies on getting above the fray to see this
more expansive view. Brian's book helped me to do this.

TED ESLER | President, Missio Nexus, author of *Innovation Crisis*

God has planted within us the seeds of growth that are designed to bear fruit
throughout our lives. Brian Sanders has written a clear, engaging tutorial describing the developmental tasks, invitations, and challenges to growth at every stage
of faith formation. *The 6 Seasons of Calling* offers readers an indispensable companion as they seek to live into a healthy, generative discipleship process every
step of the journey. Highly recommended!

MICHELLE VAN LOON | Author of *Becoming Sage: Cultivating Maturity,
Purpose, and Spirituality in Midlife*

We have all faced a painful challenge or change that stops our forward movement
like a brick wall. At that moment we wonder, can anything good come from this?
What if I'm finished? With sage wisdom, *The 6 Seasons of Calling* dismantles the
brick wall we're facing. Brian Sanders creates a liberating pathway for seeing and
discerning how God is present amidst our bewilderment. God's spirit is not only
working in our best days but in all our days! This book might be the most acces-
sible and actionable resource I've seen on navigating life's surprising journey of
beauty and brokenness. I want to give a copy of this potent book to everyone I
know that is experiencing a crisis of calling and passion!

DAN WHITE JR. | Author of *Love Over Fear*, coauthor of *The Church as Move-
ment*, and cofounder of The Kineo Center in Puerto Rico

Brian's previous books charged my conscience and challenged my imagination
for the church. His same prophetic voice comes through in *The 6 Seasons of Calling*. The framework he proposes here comes from deep reflection on his own life
and ministry. This book will help you gain perspective for your current moment
so that instead of feeling hurried or like you're trailing behind, you'll have the
courage to be present and to live into it as God intends.

DANIEL YANG | Director of the Send Institute

Most of us wish we'd had a road map to navigate the stages of our own development in our personal calling. Brian Sanders provides a road map of the six stages using Scripture, psychology, and a width of personal experience from leading one of the most innovative ministries in the West. Sanders is one of the best-read leaders the church has, and his depth of insight and ability to analyze come to bear in this seminal work that we all wish we'd had starting out. Fortunately, it's just in time for wherever you are on the journey of your own calling.

PEYTON JONES | Author of *Church Plantology: The Art and Science of Planting Churches*; founder of newbreednetwork.org

I had such deep resonance with *The 6 Seasons of Calling* that I couldn't stop talking about it. I wanted everyone to share in the wisdom gleaned in this gem. Brian has gifted us with a seminal book on the stages of calling common to all of our lives. It is as inspiring as it is insightful. An outstanding book! Highly recommended!

DEB HIRSCH | Missional leader, pastor, and author of *Redeeming Sex: Naked Conversations about Sexuality and Spirituality*

I loved Brian's book! The clarification that calling is more relational and dynamic was so helpful. The focus on conceptual language to understand and describe my own journey created a strong framework for my ongoing development and my coaching of others. I have already started to pass on what I learned from Brian's work to those I mentor, and look forward to getting this book in their hands. Brian's Day 5 calling to give away what he has been given is clearly demonstrated in his book. It truly is a gift of his own experience and wisdom that will in turn bless many!

JEFF VANDERSTELT | Author and visionary leader of Soma Family of Churches and Saturate

A renewed clarity on calling may be the most pressing need for every leader in any discipline of life. Brian has put in the hard work, and this book is a treasure for any person looking to make a legitimate contribution to the world.

HUGH HALTER | Author of *The Tangible Kingdom*

The 6 SEASONS of CALLING

DISCOVERING YOUR PURPOSE IN EACH STAGE OF LIFE

BRIAN SANDERS

MOODY PUBLISHERS
CHICAGO

All Scripture quotations, unless otherwise indicated, are taken from the Holy Bible, New International Version®, NIV®. Copyright © 1973, 1978, 1984, 2011 by Biblica, Inc.™ Used by permission of Zondervan. All rights reserved worldwide. www.zondervan.com The "NIV" and "New International Version" are trademarks registered in the United States Patent and Trademark Office by Biblica, Inc.™

Scripture quotation marked NRSV is from the New Revised Standard Version of the Bible, copyright 1989, by the Division of Christian Education of the National Council of the Churches of Christ in the USA. Used by permission. All rights reserved.

All emphasis in Scripture has been added.

A version of the section "Interlude: The Descent of Leadership" was previously published by Brian Sanders on the Medium blog: Brian Sanders, "The Descent of Leadership," June 5, 2020, https://bsunderground .medium.com.

Edited by Amanda Cleary Eastep
Interior Design: Puckett Smartt
Cover Design: Erik M. Peterson
Cover illustration of leaf copyright © 2020 by Svetsol / Shutterstock (1824306794). All rights reserved.

Library of Congress Cataloging-in-Publication Data

Names: Sanders, Brian, 1972- author.
Title: The six seasons of calling : discovering your purpose in each stage
   of life / Brian Sanders.
Description: Chicago : Moody Publishers, [2022] | Includes bibliographical
   references. | Summary: "This book helps you view your calling as ongoing
   and dynamic. God has ordained six seasons as your life unfolds:
   childhood, adolescence, early career, mid-career, late career, and
   transition. Instead of wandering aimlessly through life, let the six
   seasons of calling provide structure for the life God has for you"--
   Provided by publisher.
Identifiers: LCCN 2021034557 (print) | LCCN 2021034558 (ebook) | ISBN
   9780802423948 | ISBN 9780802499783 (ebook)
Subjects: LCSH: Christianity--Psychology. | Developmental
   psychology--Religious aspects--Christianity. | Vocation--Christianity.
Classification: LCC BR110 .S328 2022 (print) | LCC BR110 (ebook) | DDC
   261.5/15--dc23
LC record available at https://lccn.loc.gov/2021034557
LC ebook record available at https://lccn.loc.gov/2021034558

Originally delivered by fleets of horse-drawn wagons, the affordable paperbacks from D. L. Moody's publishing house resourced the church and served everyday people. Now, after more than 125 years of publishing and ministry, Moody Publishers' mission remains the same—even if our delivery systems have changed a bit. For more information on other books (and resources) created from a biblical perspective, go to www.moodypublishers.com or write to:

Moody Publishers
820 N. LaSalle Boulevard
Chicago, IL 60610

1 3 5 7 9 10 8 6 4 2

Printed in the United States of America

For Eve.

For reminding me that our lives are more than one season.

CONTENTS

THE FINGERPRINT PARADOX

All the world's a stage,
And all the men and women merely players;
They have their exits and entrances,
And one man in his time plays many parts,
His acts being seven ages.[1]

Life is full of paradoxes. So it is that in a calling, we find that each person is utterly unique; yet, there are common, recurring patterns in all our lives. We are all born. We are all children before we are adults. We all suffer grief and loss. We all face limitations, and if we are healthy, eventually we come to terms with those limitations. The bigger the struggle, the easier it is to agree on its commonality. We all want to be loved, for instance, yet the shape and dimension that love will take in our lives is as individual as each of us. Even the gospel, which is good news for all of us, slides into our ears at the exact angle of our need. What makes the good news of Jesus and the kingdom He has promised so utterly engrossing is precisely this fact. Like a great banquet, there is so much on the table, it will assuredly satiate every hunger. But everyone regards the feast through the bias and the hunger of their own existential need.

This is how He finds us, at the point of that need; the awareness of that hunger. And I hear the good news, in that sense, for me. He can save us all precisely because He knows us *all*. The secret of evangelism is that the gospel is never heard or received in exactly the same way. And this is its power: to offer one word that can save us all precisely because it is the same *and* it is different.

They say no two fingerprints are the same. But all fingers leave a print. They offer a unique pattern, but the patterns are remarkably similar. Maybe every soul is like that too. No two lives are the same. Let's get that settled right away. I want to make some observations about our commonality, but those will only ultimately be helpful to you if you remember this companion truth behind every assertion.

As much as we defend our individuality, the search for those common patterns is a kind of obsession for us. We love to see patterns (real or imagined) in our shared human story. Personality typologies are perhaps the best example of this. Far from being pure science, these versions of Jungian archetypes are completely based on observation. Frameworks like Myers-Briggs Type Indicator, the DiSC Assessment, the Enneagram, et al., are all reflections on observable patterns. But they are also full of confirmation bias; we see in them a version of ourselves we are willing to see.

Admitting that does not invalidate the typology—it unveils its real value.

You see, these systems are not best used definitively; that is, to define who we are as people. They are best used communally in order to give us a shared language for understanding the ways we are the same and the ways we are different. In other words, it does not so much matter if they fully define the vastness of human personality; they give us a way of comprehending and talking about that vastness, and most profoundly, a way of embracing the paradox that we are the same *and* we are different.

For while we like to believe we are each special, that truth can also be isolating and even frightening. Some of our most destructive pathologies are rooted in an exaggerated sense of uniqueness. To believe, for instance, that God loves all people, forgives all people, but just not me, is a kind of insecurity that is a lot like its sister, pride. Conversely, to believe God loves me more and needs to forgive me less than He does other people is basically the same malady. So it is that the tributaries of both pride and insecurity are mutations of uniqueness. When we are feeling proud, we need the balancing of commonality to humble us. When we are feeling flawed and insecure, we likewise need the balance of shared human experience to lift us. You are not alone in the experience of this life. And yet you experience it in a way that is utterly unique to you.

Finding these common patterns is primarily the work of observation. There will always be limits to those observations, as well as people and places that may not fit the pattern. I offer this modest contribution to the search for those common patterns based on two mitigating factors.

First, the scope of my reflection is limited to our lifelong pursuit of our calling. I am not looking at development through some other lens or concern, which would certainly influence the conclusions I might draw. Instead, I am trying to observe that elusive sense of what it is that God wants us to be doing with our lives at any given moment.

Second, this comes from my work over the last twenty years helping hundreds of people discover and discern the direction of God for their lives at various stages. I write from my conviction of faith. Just as I have searched for the invisible hand of God at work in the seasons of my own life, I have also seen Him at work in others'.

Just as playwright William Shakespeare would see the seven ages of man and compare them to acts in a play, or medieval mystic Teresa of Ávila would see seven mansions of the heart unlocked in prayer, so it is that we see certain patterns through the lens we bring. This is not a liability to the process, but rather a gift. As long as we can see the bias, we can appreciate its value in the overall catalog of developmental templates.

There is precedent for this kind of ordered observation. Each new vantage point, rather than closing the book on the study of life cycle and psychosocial development, inspires deeper work. Each exploring growth and development from a perspective that we need. I am indebted to these models, if not for their conclusions, then for their construction.

FRAMEWORKS

Erik Erikson was a German-American psychologist whose emphasis on childhood development lead him to uncover eight stages of psychosocial development.[2] These stages offer us age equivalencies for comparison, and look to uncover both the virtue and crisis of each age group. This kind of reflection is remarkable as it sounds the depths of our common experience, as well as the inner challenges each stage brings. Still, his work is excessively Freudian and leans heavily on early childhood development and adolescence, perhaps underestimating the massive changes that occur in us later in life (five of his eight stages occur before the age of nineteen). You can see his framework here.

Erik Erikson's Stages of Psychosocial Development[3]

GROUP	AGE	VIRTUE	CRISIS
INFANTS	0 to 18 mo	Hope	Trust vs. Mistrust
TODDLERS	18 mo to 3 yrs	Will	Autonomy vs. Shame & Doubt
PRESCHOOL	3 to 6 yrs	Purpose	Initiative vs. Guilt
CHILDHOOD	6 to 12 yrs	Competence	Industry vs. Inferiority
ADOLESCENCE	12 to 18 yrs	Fidelity	Identity vs. Role Confusion
YOUNG ADULTS	19 to 40 yrs	Love	Intimacy vs. Isolation
MIDDLE ADULTHOOD	40 to 64 yrs	Care	Generativity vs. Stagnation
SENIORS	65 yrs +	Wisdom	Ego Intergrity vs. Despair

American theologian James Fowler offers us six stages of faith.[4] By contrast, his framework gives no age equivalences, instead laying out an observable cognitive journey. His work has given dimension to the otherwise enigmatic realm of faith. These stages not only demystify the relationship of faith and maturity, they ease the tension that relationship implicitly creates. While I do not agree completely with his conclusions, I find the template incredibly stimulating. At least, it urges me to ask new and important questions, at best, it comforts me in my own journey of faith, doubt, and growth.

James Fowler's Stages of Faith[5]

STAGE	TITLE	STAGE OF LIFE	DESCRIPTION
0	Primal or Undifferentiated	Infant/Toddler	Early learning of the safety of the environment (warm, safe, and secure vs. hurt, neglect, and abuse) seeds of faith/spirituality
1	Intuitive-Projective	Preschool	Need for concrete symbols and stories
2	Mythic-Literal	School Age	Strong beliefs in the justice/reciprocity of the universe. Deities are almost always anthropomorphic
3	Synthetic-Conventional	Adolescence	Conformity to a personal myth, identity, set of values
4	Individuative-Reflective	Early Adulthood	Taking of personal responsibility for beliefs, values, systems of meaning, commitments
5	Conjunctive	Middle Adulthood	Acknowledgment of paradoxes of experience. Faith subjected to critical reflection (1st/2nd naivete)
6	Universalizing	Adult	Altruistically creating of zones of liberation

Understanding this body of work helps us see that while there may not be one single pattern to describe our common journey, there are discernable patterns that overlap to reveal some kind of shared experience. These can be deeply enriching and give us real insight into our lives. I have been personally impacted and inspired by the Grant Study, the most comprehensive longitudinal study in history.[6] George Vaillant's breathtaking work examines what is now a 70 plus–year study of 268 Harvard students, first enrolled in the late 1930s. The sheer ambition of the project, chasing key metrics over so long, is fascinating. However, what is even more remarkable is how the science behind the study has itself changed over that same period. Data thought crucial in 1940 has become obsolete, while other factors have emerged, leaving no doubt that the researcher influences the research. Still, this kind of commitment to the belief that such a study will (and does) uncover evidence of our common struggle is inspiring. And interestingly enough, this vast study comes to a most profound and simple conclusion about love, something we will revisit at the end of these reflections.

These examples serve as evidence of our obsession to find some sameness in our difference. In that spirit, I offer the following framework on the stages of calling I've developed.

Six Days of Developmental Calling

DAY	AGE	CORE DEVELOPMENTAL CONCEPT	IDEAL DEVELOPMENTAL CONDITION	PRIMARY DEVELOPMENTAL THREAT	CALLING & IDENTITY
1 Childhood	0 to 12	Bonding	Play	Fear & Isolation	Child
2 Adolescence	12 to 24	Learning	Agency	Inversion	Student
3 Early Career	24 to 36	Serving	Challenge	Entitlement & Impatience	Worker
4 Mid Career	36 to 48	Creating	Impact	Greed	Maker
5 Late Career	48 to 60	Giving	Scale	Distraction	Mentor
6 Transition	60 to 72	Finishing	Celebration	Obscurity	Mystic

In this book, I posit that each person's life, like the world created for us, is shaped and made by God over six distinct periods of time. Of course, these stages, which make up the Six Days of our lives (column 1), will take on the one-of-a-kind contours of our individual experience. But, in an attempt to find some semblance of our common developmental story, I will outline six features. An age range (column 2) is important to engage and locate our current developmental moment. Further, by attaching ages to these "days," we are able to review the past through the lens of these ideas.

As it relates to calling, the focus will be on what growth looks like in each stage (Core Developmental Concept), the conditions necessary for that development to take place (ideal for flourishing), and the primary threat to that development. This will provide the rubric for my analysis and discussion of each Day.

Additionally, these Days are meant to represent not just our developmental journey, but our listening posture in the key moments of our lives. The single most important generative act of our faith is surrender—the delivering of our lives to the lordship of Jesus. And because we understand that Jesus is not just a figure from history or a spirit to be embodied, we must remember that He is very much a living being who has accepted our fealty. More than that, He has promised to be an active leader and participant in our lives. So it is that we do not develop alone. Our great mentor and model walks with us through every developmental Day, calling us in new ways to faithfulness to Him and His cause.

Further, because Jesus' work in us is a cumulative work, the gains of each Day are not lost. This cumulative implication is important to keep in the forefront as we walk through these stages. We do not lose the gifts of the previous Days; they stay with us and we build upon them. The status of a child stays with us. So too the learning and questioning of the adolescent and the servanthood of early career are qualities we never abandon. We simply add to them.

Here, Erikson's idea that each stage is "developmentally indispensable for later stages"[7] is so valuable. These Days are interconnected and a part of one wonderful story of growth and maturation (holiness). The sad companion then to culmination is regression. If we are meant to build on the lessons and virtues that each Day delivers, then it is also possible to fall back into their struggles and vices. And we often do. An ancillary value of this kind of outline is that we can see the way forward. Having said that, regression is not always bad. It can be that we need to renew or remember the lessons and natural calling of the previous Days. But we are not meant to stay there long. Maturity always awaits us in the future; and stagnation is always the enemy of life and growth.

Finally, here are a few words of advice in reading this book:

These are not precise lengths of time. Don't get too hung up on that. Look for the pattern in your own life and development. And maybe most importantly, locate yourself in the sequence and look for what might be next.

Don't get discouraged if you feel a sense of loss or regret. We will all be reading this having passed the development season of multiple Days. You can learn from that loss, note it, and also try to recapture some aspects of it later in life. There is nothing stopping you from going through an accelerated version of these developmental milestones in the future.

Having said that, **don't imagine you can do it faster than everyone else.** (The achiever types will tend to put themselves in that category.) This *is* the accelerated version. The framework represents a well-lived life. Even the most ambitious person cannot rush time and the lessons it teaches us. You may be able, for example, to accelerate learning and put a fourteen-year-old in college, but only at a cost to the fourteen-year-old. We understand implicitly that to lose a portion of our childhood in the name of achievement is often a Faustian bargain. We know that precisely because our childhood has now passed, and we only now see its full value. So it is with the other Days of development. Only at the end of our lives will we see exactly why each of these was valuable in their own way and not to have been rushed.

Pray as you go. At times I will be explicit about hearing the voice of God in this process. Even though there will be sections of the book in which that more mystical reality falls into the background, its importance never changes. The yearning behind our desire to know ourselves and make sense of our lives is really a yearning for intimate relationship with God. Carry that with you as you read and reflect and this will not just be a journey of learning but a journey of loving encounter.

Finally, **consider the caution and encouragement on stage theory** from psychologist David Benner in his book *Surrender to Love*:

> The danger of any stage theory is that it suggests a mechanical and linear movement through a process. Clearly life does not unfold in this way. A delineation of stages might also suggest work to be undertaken or tasks to be accomplished. But such work would inevitably be in the service of the ego and not genuinely transformational. Growth in love is not an accomplishment but the receipt of a gift. However, if stages are not interpreted in an overly literal fashion they can be helpful in understanding the process of our growth in love. And if we can resist the temptation to turn them into something we do to achieve a desired end, they can help us focus on God, who is the source of any genuine transformation.[8]

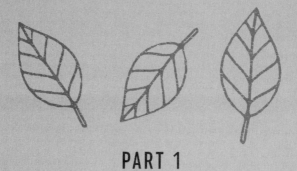

PART 1

DYNAMIC
CALLING

DYNAMIC CALLING

It took God six days to make the world. Six, somehow distinct, passages of time. Getting caught up in the duration of those "days" seems less wondrous to me than the underlying implication: it took more than one. There is something profoundly important about this first lesson from God as Creator and craftsperson. Creation is a process.

He took His time.

In those opening words, we also learn that He made us in His image. Male and female He created us, presumably to create as well. Perhaps part of what it means to be created in the image of God is that we too are given six metaphorical days to create something good, complex, and beautiful—to enter into our rest, surveying all that we have done and being able to say... it was good.

Surely we can agree our lives are also the culmination of a process. In some strange partnership, it seems our lives are both the product of our own creative freedom and His ongoing creative impetus. Those of us who have pledged our lives to Jesus live as a "new creation" (2 Cor. 5:17), "created in Christ Jesus to do good works" (Eph. 2:10). We are given our own span of Six Days to create and be re-created. Our individual lives stand as potential works of art, changing and growing into His likeness. But we too are makers. Our lives can do work, as He did, creating something that was not there before. Then, when we finally rest from all our labor, that work will be left behind as a legacy gift to those who would come after us.

LIFE AS PROCESS

Your life is a process. You are not what you once were and you are not what you will yet become. These two truths are the basis for Christian hope. God is still at work, creating us and creating through us. The New Testament offers us the beautiful idea and often invisible work of sanctification; that ever-present contact with the living presence of God. In our time, we have taken to calling it growth, which is also a nice way of saying it. But the more ancient idea of sanctification, to make something holy, gives more modern words like growth and development needed dimension. We are meant to grow and develop. But why? For what purpose? "For those God foreknew he also predestined to be conformed to the image of his Son" (Rom. 8:29).

Missiologically, this means God wants people set loose in the world who think, act, and feel like His Son. We are sent by God to represent Jesus, but we are works in progress in reflecting Him. So, we are changed (sanctified) to better reveal Him. But developmentally, we are also being prepared for eternity. That is, we are being remade for union too. Because this kind of growth is often painful, it helps to see it as preparation for something. And it hurts a bit less when we realize it is the loving presence of God at work in us, reshaping and redeeming the pain of our lives to reveal His Son and prepare us for eternity. However you analyze it, we have all been given our own span of days to create, to make something with our lives. But we are also being made into something through the process of living. God is always there, using us, yes, but also recreating and making us as we go.

LIFE AS LONGING

I am convinced that the two greatest longings of the human heart are for intimacy and purpose. We all (whether we admit it or not) need to be known, wanted, and loved. This is only possible in relationship with something or someone outside of ourselves. Let's call that the longing for *intimacy*. Simultaneously, we all need to believe we matter, that our lives are significant in some way, not useless, futile, or inconsequential. Let's call that a longing for *purpose*. Elegantly, the truest satisfaction of those two longings are found in the same place. Calling.

Calling implies two corresponding realities. First, there is someone who calls. And what can you know about that One who calls? The God who calls you is also the One who created you. The God who calls you also called His Son to die for you. In other words, the One who calls you has twice loved you, in both creation and sacrifice. His longing is for you, and so He calls. When I call for one of my kids, it means I want them to come to me. It is deeply relational. It means, of course, I know them by name. But it also means I want them. Think about that. To be known and wanted is implicit in hearing any call from God. Further, calling means that drawing near is not just something you initiate. He initiates with you. Calling implies the deepest possible intimacy with the greatest possible person.

The One who calls you has twice loved you, in both creation and sacrifice.

Second, calling implies that there is something He wants you to do. Only you. Significance and purpose, then, offer a secondary implication of calling. We like the idea of "knowing our calling" because we want to know what to do with our lives. We want to be good at something; we wonder what will bring us the greatest job satisfaction or personal fulfillment. And perhaps it will, but only if it is coupled with the intimacy that is offered at first. To know and operate from a place of gifting and talent without a relationship with the One who designed and gifted you is to feel a special kind of emptiness. An emptiness that comes from being so close to something, to sense it is near, but never close enough to touch or hold. Purpose then, is something connected to *His* will and wishes in the world. God is still at work, through His people, announcing and ushering in His kingdom; and to be a part of that in any way is its own reward. Conversely, to be good at something—to walk skillfully through the world while divorcing that ability from the ultimate purposes of God—is to fall just short of a full life.[1]

It is therefore impossible to live into the fullness of your purpose—to flourish through the developmental Days of your life—without intimacy with your Father and without clarity on the part you are meant to play in His purposes. If you hope to see your life reach its full potential, you must draw close to the One who designed you and sends you into the world He loves. We all have a part yet to play in the coming of His kingdom. Just as finding intimacy in the face of Jesus is the greatest possible intimacy, so finding purpose in the mission of Jesus is the greatest possible purpose.

STATIC AND DYNAMIC CALLING

One problem we must then confront has to do with the nature of our calling. Is it something that happens only once in our lives? Whether conscious or not, we often think about calling as something static and unchanging. Thinking about calling in this way, as a singular event, not only weighs it down with tremendous anxiety (as in I had better get it right), but it causes us to procrastinate coming to a conclusion. In the early years of our weekend calling experience, which we named the Calling Lab, I used to think that someone could just lock themselves away in the place of prayer and hear God tell them what they were called to. We learned quickly that it was never quite so simple. While people can and do hear God in the place of prayer, what they hear is rarely as specific as we imagined it would be. Further, as we walked with the same people through the years, we began to see that those nudges from God, when they did come, were often only true for a time. They would often evolve through the complexity of the lives of people who heard them. For instance, a young woman might hear a call to advocacy for children, which at first takes the form of systemic action, but then evolves into something more localized once she has kids of her own. Calling in that way is adaptive and responsive to the major changes of our lives.

I was a hyperactive child. I had trouble sitting still and found the ever-present class directive to listen in silence pretty close to impossible. Coupled with my authority issues, I was often in trouble and my grades were poor. School simply was not a place I ever did well. This might be why I can remember so vividly the first time I was praised by a teacher. It was fifth grade and we were asked to give a speech about someone from history. I am not sure why, but I chose Julius Caesar. I fashioned a makeshift bedsheet toga, slid on my mother's sandals, and took my place at the front of the class.

When I had finished, I can still remember the long, shocked pause from my teacher as she searched for what to say. She settled on some version of the sentiment, "Well, now, Brian, that was actually not bad." No one was more surprised than I was. It was not just the rarified air of affirmation that lived on in my memory, but the feeling I had just before her assessment. The feeling of *knowing* that I had done well, even before she said anything. That feeling of finding something that for others is hard but for you is easy. This is not just a clue to calling; it is evidence of the work of God in us. You see, we are desperate sinners, corrupting as much as we nurture. We are all deeply selfish and even dangerous in the right (or wrong) conditions. So, to find something that you can do that is not like that, that is somehow good for the world, that somehow reflects back to the grace (*charis*/gift) of God at work in the world through you, is truly magical.

There was a clue, even then, to my calling. Though I could not recognize it yet, I was hearing the voice of God. Still, I was not ultimately called to give historical speeches to ten-year-olds. This was only a clue. But an important clue. If we think about calling as something static, as something one-dimensional, we miss the way it is meant to grow and change with us. If what we do is one dimension, then how we do it changes over the second dimension of time.

In other words, we have to think about calling as something that interacts and intersects with our life-long development. We are always changing. The circumstances of our lives are always changing. The quality of our character, our skill, wisdom, and maturity changes the way in which we execute our calling. In short, calling is something that is meant to grow and change with us. Calling is dynamic.

CALLING OVER TIME

The first revelation for me was that we are all called. Not just some of us, all of us. The second revelation was that our calling is not something that happens to us once. It is something that changes with the changes of our lives. But the third revelation is just as significant: *calling is something that changes but also lasts.* I contend that your calling will materially change about six times over the course of your life. But whether you agree fully with my proposal or not, calling is not a single event, and it is likewise not something that should be revisited every year.

Again, it is important to remember that calling is not a

disembodied or impersonal idea. It is fundamentally relational. In other words, calling is dynamic because God is dynamic and your relationship with God is dynamic. But calling also requires fidelity to a course of action, because God gives us assignments that require persevering obedience. I am convinced that God does want to give us the experience of what Friedrich Nietzsche called "a long obedience in the same direction,"[2] while continually calling us back to Himself. How then can we know when enough time has passed and our calling might be changing?

THE CALLING CYCLE

The search for calling usually begins with a crisis. That crisis could be big or small. It could be something external or something internal, and it could be something good or something bad. It could be something that we do to ourselves, such as failing or succeeding; or it could be something that happens to us, like a loss or an opportunity. But behind the cause lies the true crisis, which is one of identity. The college freshman who has to pick a major; the college graduate who no longer has school to define their existence; the young careerist who has just lost their first job or been promoted to a better one; the parents who are sending their last child off to college; or the husband who is burying his wife. All of these people are sharing, not one experience, but an inception of the same crisis of identity. Who am I now? Who am I if I am not a student? An employee? A parent of kids at home? A spouse?

It is in this crisis of identity that we are tempted by fear and despair, but also driven into the presence of God. I cannot say how many times something like this will happen in your life, but it will happen. And it will happen more than once. Again, I am making the case that for most of us, it will happen about six times. And that is normal, healthy, and to be expected. As a follower of Jesus, these moments of identity crisis can and should become the catalyst for a renewal, not so much of our current calling, but of our relationship with the Father.

The beautiful and painful question "Who am I now?" not only seeks an answer, it seeks an answerer. Perhaps what we need most is to know that there is someone who can (and has always been able to) answer it. So, the identity crisis is meant to drive us into intimacy with Jesus, to seek His face, and to find there, not just the answer to our questions, but the One who defines all that we are.

> The beautiful and painful question "Who am I now?" not only seeks an answer, it seeks an answerer.

The identity crisis drives us to intimacy and prayer. And it is in the place of prayer, Scripture reading, listening, and hearing His still, small voice, that we come again back to ourselves. We hear again His words over us, "You are . . . " Often, that word is very much a renewal of something He has said to us before, reviving our previous sense of calling and pushing us back into the same fight, the same work, and the same hope. Still, there is always something new that is conferred. Even if that new thing is simply deeper conviction. From identity comes purpose: "You are . . ." therefore, "Go and do . . ." Almost certainly this is where we will experience real change in the contours of our calling. Perhaps the change is subtle, but it could very likely be something big. And so we venture out again, in faith, into that work He has called us to do. From my perspective, that too, will last about twelve years. And then we will find ourselves again, bored, ineffective, limited, or facing some truly new situation that will begin the cycle again.

The Calling Cycle

You can see why experiencing this every month or even every year would not only be destabilizing, but it would not allow us to accomplish much with our lives. You can also see how going through this cycle only once or even twice in our lives would not really reflect the bigger changes and challenges we each must face. So it is that we will all search and find our calling several times in our lives.

CALLING AS CULMINATION

Over the Six Days of our lives, calling will look different because in each Day the demands of growth and development are different. Each of our callings are unique, but the process of being called and responding to that dynamic calling is remarkably similar. Before you can be a professional athlete, you must first learn the fundamentals, learn your own strengths and weaknesses compared to other players, build a body of experience, and practice until you achieve mastery. So too with your own life. You are growing for a purpose. Every failure, every mistake, every hard fought lesson, and every apparent success has value if it is integrated and repurposed for something greater.

Of course we are playing all of these roles throughout the stages of our lives, but having a sense of what is first or essential can relieve some of the anxiety as we search for meaning and identity. This is hard because just as you get the hang of living in a certain Day, things seem to change. What worked for you (and was often hard to settle into) becomes foreign or just off in the new Day. Calling changes, because we change. Remember my Julius Caesar moment? God might have been calling me to be a ministry leader, but He wasn't calling me to be one while I was in fifth grade. Still, because of that call, He first called me to lead through communication, something that would be developed in me even when I was not living for Him.

So, while we change and the context of our lives changes, there is often a thread of focus that stays with us. Is this what we mean when we say words like vocation and calling? I think so. But you may not be able to see it fully until it is behind you. You must then live in the fullness of the Day you are in. In time, a bigger picture may well emerge.

I offer six stages because I am convinced that the "just right" Goldilocks principle applies to the twelve-year period. It is just long enough to really live into a calling but not so long that we lose our zeal or contextual relevance. I am also convinced of the markers I will share, the transition points in our development that occur right around these increments of twelve. This template has been confirmed for me time and again in the lives of the people who have come to us trying to discern their calling. Still, no developmental map like this can fit every life, and each person's journey is unique. In the next section we will take these six seasons one at a time, unpacking the dynamics of calling and growth and the forces that keep us from both. Try to locate your own story, but also to notice the ways that your story might deviate from the pattern. Both discoveries can become raw material for your own self-discovery and ultimately for hearing God speaking to you about your past, your present, and your future.

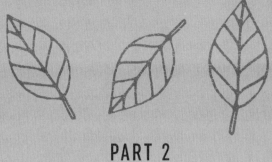

PART 2

THE SIX DAYS OF CALLING

DAY 1

THE CHILD

*"Truly I tell you, anyone who will not receive the kingdom of God like
a little child will never enter it." And he took the children in his arms,
placed his hands on them and blessed them.*

MARK 10:15-16

CHILDHOOD: BIRTH TO 12

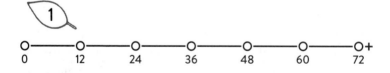

E arly childhood development is a wonderfully complex field.
As we venture into it, I need to limit the scope of our inquiry
to calling, specifically the word that God gives us and the task
He sets upon us (our mission) in each life stage. Applying this
idea to early childhood may seem strange and even misplaced.
After all, what toddler needs to be thinking about their calling?
This reluctance reveals that already we have misunderstood a

central implication of calling. Fredrick Buechner famously said, "The place God calls you to is the place where your deep gladness and the world's deep hunger meet."[1]

I have already made the argument that calling is about a relationship with God. It is hearing from Him; first, that we are known, loved, and wanted, and then, important enough to warrant some assignment. This certainly applies to children. From the moment we draw breath, we are called by God into His gracious work in the world. Using the more helpful notion of dynamic calling, we can begin to consider what that might look like in a life that is so new to this world.

The Bible does not give us much on the experience of childhood. There is plenty to read about the poor, the small, and the overlooked. We can certainly transfer principles of God's concern for the poor to children; the biblical writers likely would have seen children in the same light. In that sense, it is their vulnerability that makes them particularly important to God. Still, as we reflect on childhood, it is a mistake to remember it primarily as a time of vulnerability. That is an adult perspective superimposed on childhood. Safety and security may well be our modern collective parental obsession, but our children do not naturally experience life in that way. Children are not meant to understand and define the boundaries of their existence in terms of exposure or vulnerability. If you think back, you likely didn't either.

Still, childhood is exactly that: fragile, vulnerable, and exposed. Here is the paradox of risk in childhood development. Children are vulnerable but should never know it. There is a wonderful distinction between danger and adventure. A thriving childhood is free from mortal danger but flush with adventure.

BLESSED ARE THE SMALL

In the Bible, there are a few, almost incidental, interactions between Jesus and children. Apparently, children were among the people constantly crowding around Him. Common to each of these stories is a strong correction from Jesus to the adults trying to manage them. Presumably some of the chastened were parents. The children in each of these stories seem to be (as we may well remember our own childhoods) adventurous.

They were probably not hovering near Jesus to learn. It is unlikely these were little theological protégés. They were not there to be healed or because they needed something from Him (except for His blessing). At least we have no reason to believe that, because no such reason is given. They were not there to lure Him into a religious trap. It takes a while for human beings to become Pharisees. So what was their motivation to be around Him? What was it about Jesus that intimidated His rivals, exposed His friends, but attracted children?

Likely, they wanted what all kids want: to be close to those who love them. It is as innocent and beautiful as it is selfish. There is a clue here to a more timeless trait of childhood—the longing to bond.

Just as each Day changes, so too the key developmental concepts, the ideal conditions for thriving, and the primary threats to us in that season of life.

CORE DEVELOPMENTAL CONCEPT FOR DAY 1

BONDING

Bonding then is a conflation of the longing for adventure and the longing for intimacy. Healthy kids find the world to be a place full of both adventure and friendship. Our first friends should be our parents. The first job a newborn baby has (besides breathing) is to "latch" on to its mother. Sustenance, warmth, nurture, and visual and even psychological stimulation are all at stake in that first labor of love. The crying in the night, separation anxiety, and clinging that almost all of us exhibit aren't things to fix. On the contrary, these behaviors are evidence that babies are masters of their own developmental needs. Still, as we grow so too our sense of adventure and our need to bond with others. The world is there to be explored, not as a perilous place, but as a place that is full of good surprises. The best environment then for children to grow, develop and thrive are curated for minimal danger and maximum adventure.

If I ask you to think about the best moments of your own childhood, you might recall adventure with friends or family. The bonds that were formed stay with us long after even those memories have faded. Bonding then, is an opportunity and occasion for both play and playmates. The work of childhood is bonding. This single achievement undergirds all that we hope to be and do.

IDEAL DEVELOPMENT CONDITION FOR DAY 1

PLAY

The deep work of childhood is bonding and one of the primary pathways for bonding to occur, is play. The objects of play then are, as Erik Erikson would describe, microsphere and macrosphere.[2] In the macrosphere (playing with people), play is a conduit for connection, socialization, and forming human bonds. But in the microsphere (playing with toys), we are also able to explore and experience the world as adventure, cultivating imagination, hope, and constructiveness.

Researchers in the biological study of play, Kerrie Graham and Gordon Burghardt contend, "Play is the only known human activity that we engage in solely for the purpose of joy."[3] We can enjoy eating, procreation, achievement, etc., but all of those things are commingled with other goals. Play alone is solely about joy. Just as childhood is a non-anxious condition of children, play is something kids do naturally and without self-consciousness. Stuart Brown, founder of the National Institute of Play, has argued that play is "part of the natural instincts that children possess."[4]

I would argue that the primary goal of play is not to learn about, or even discover, the world; it is to connect with it. Before we can contrive meaning from the world, we must first belong to it. Bonding (as opposed to the Day 2 core concept of learning) is the key developmental work. We experience the world as a place filled with people, and as we bond with those people, we come to feel as though we belong. Yet, because bonding is the goal, that "work" is really play. So to belong, we bond, and to bond, we play. This is perhaps why Erickson calls this the "play age" and argues that "playfulness is an essential ingredient in all the stages to come."[5] And "in playfulness is grounded also, all sense of humor, man's specific gift to laugh at himself as well as at others."[6] At the heart of humor and playfulness is a tool we are meant to master in childhood and never abandon. Leonard Sweet, in his book *The Well-Played Life*, offers us a taxonomy of life in three ages, each of which is defined by a relationship to play.[7] Playfulness, as a disposition, helps us to see the world as essentially relational. While principle, pettiness, and conflict will threaten to separate us, we will struggle to walk in our creative calling if we cannot continue to play and bond with other human beings.

PRIMARY DEVELOPMENTAL THREAT FOR DAY 1

FEAR AND ISOLATION

The conditions that would most damage our call to childhood would, therefore, be conditions that inhibit bonding and restrict meaningful play. Early human contact is critical for not only psychological development, but physical, social, and spiritual development, as well. We do not need research to tell us that babies who experience affection, intimacy, and deep connection with their parents are better off than those who don't.

There is almost an ontological urge in all of us to bond with children. We know they need it, but maybe so do we. The natural love and affection parents feel in the presence of their children is as profound as it is telling. Normally self-centered people are suddenly making heroic promises to these tiny vulnerable versions of themselves. It is as strong an evidence of the *imago Dei* as anything in anthropology. Still, those same promises are abandoned soon enough as sin and circumstance intrude on our best intentions. The drive to bond may be there, but so too the threat of abandonment and abuse. Kids who thrive are those who have been able to quickly and thoroughly bond with their parents, their siblings, and in time their friends.

Kids who are orphaned face developmental challenges. Likewise, children whose childhoods mirror orphanhood in various ways, such as physical and/or emotional neglect, face similar challenges. Because bonding is the key developmental concept, anything that breaks relationship becomes a clear and present danger to the calling of the child. Abandonment, emotional distance, withholding physical contact, all forms of abuse, and even relational divergence by proxy (like divorce, or having siblings taken from the home) all become serious threats to the child's development.

If the natural creative work of bonding is play, then the natural destructive work of bonding is abuse. Direct violence to the body or psyche of a child does not only do immediate harm to them (as well as leave psychological scars), it undermines the ongoing possibility of meaningful relationship. It communicates that bonding is dangerous. To be close to someone can get us hurt. And while that is a true lesson that life will fully and finally teach us, it is not one that a child should be learning. The bonds formed are meant to form a kind of immunity to that very reality that will certainly visit us later in life. This is why bonding through play (relationships built on the pursuit of mutual joy) lay a foundation for a persistent hope throughout the relational brokenness and challenges of adulthood.

Even though relational brokenness and the conditions that surround it can produce fear of intimacy and ultimately isolation, kids are further limited when those experiences are projected onto the whole of life. Strangely, even the fear of fear itself can creep into the psyche of both parents and children. When relational breakdown is everywhere, sometimes parents, and in turn kids, can try to avoid any danger, risk, or pain at all. This can result in yet another kind of isolation, not just from people but from the world around us. The parent who cannot imagine taking the risk of allowing their kids to walk to school may inadvertently teach their kids that the world outside is scary and unpredictable. Excessive caution sometimes has the unintended consequence of multiplying fear.

The greater problem in childhood development is not that the world is an unsafe place, it is that we teach our kids to think of it as an unsafe place.[8] This is essentially the challenge of parenting a child: to protect children from real danger and serious harm while simultaneously giving them a sense that the world is basically wonderful, unpredictable, and interesting. In other words, of all the threats to the safety of children, fear may be the biggest. If parents create a cocoon of fear, they damage their children's sense of hope and connectedness.

I grew up in Florida, swimming in rivers and closely interacting with alligators. Our parents taught us to respect them but not fear them. I am still comfortable swimming in water where there are alligators nearby because I know that I am not in real danger.

In contrast, the almost overwhelming fear people have of these animals arises, not from experience or even research, but from the sensational and rare stories we have heard, which likely only reached us precisely because they were fear inducing. The best environments give us just enough room to learn and get hurt but not damaged beyond repair, to learn to respect the world around us but not fear it. If we give in to a worldview of existential danger, we can't fully play; and if we can't play, we will not bond.[9] This is why both rational fear (as an understandable outcome of abuse) or irrational fear (as a worldview of over-caution) will isolate us, inhibiting play and bonding.

CALLING AND IDENTITY IN DAY 1

TO BE A CHILD

Jesus said, "Let the little children come to me, and do not hinder them, for the kingdom of heaven belongs to such as these" (Matt. 19:14). I am very moved by the rich meaning of the Greek word that gets translated here as "belong." It is the word *pros* (πρός), which is where we get the utilitarian prefix for things like pro-life, or pro-union. It means to advantage, to favor, to be set up in such a way as to be more fitting for a certain kind of person or idea.[10] The kingdom then, is pro-children. It is set up for them.

Jesus' fondness for the children He came in contact with, and their way of being, immediately became an apt illustration of the kingdom. To be like a child, in some mysterious way, is what we are all supposed to be striving for. It is the only way to enter into and take part in the kingdom (Matt. 19:13–14;

18:1–5). So it is that childhood is not a missionless season of our lives. Instead, it is a foundational time when we are called to be exactly what it is easiest to be, a child. Children already belong to the kingdom, representing it, even bearing witness to it in some unconscious way.

Most early childhood development theories would break down this Day into more than a single time segment. There are surely big shifts in the life of a child from infant to toddler and then to school age. There are major developmental milestones that I am overlooking because when it comes to calling (what it is that God is asking a child to do), it generally is the same until puberty.

There is an innocence traditionally afforded to children. We have long understood that their physical and cognitive development is so radical before the age of twelve that we can hardly hold them eternally accountable for their actions. We do not judge children the same way we judge adults. They are not capable of crime in the same way; we understand that they are essentially in a perpetual state of becoming.

When Jesus says, let the children come, He might also be saying, let them explore the world as a place of adventure and not a place of restriction. In turn, when He says, you must become like one of these little ones to enter the kingdom, He is saying, among other things, that what they are is enough. It may be the only time in our lives when what we are is all we need to be.

Unlike all the other Days of calling, this one has almost certainly already passed for each of us. Seeing this pattern now is a great benefit to the children who are in our lives today but could also feel like a bitter pill for those of us who experienced less than ideal childhoods. If the latter is true, I would encourage you to find a way to recapture some of these lost conditions. It may not be the Day you are in now, but there are features of this first Day, which if never experienced, need to be cultivated even now if we are to develop into wholehearted human beings.

If you never experienced adventure or play, take an improv class or volunteer with the kids' program at your church. Find ways to cultivate that. If you know that you failed to bond, talk to someone about that. Double back and spend some time and energy finding ways to do just that. It is never too late. These are conditions we need to build on. Even if we have to find them later in life, we can do that in order to grow beyond them.

The writers of the New Testament will go on to understand childhood as an essential and foundational theological construct. We are all meant to know ourselves, perpetually as children of God.[11] For that is what we are. Conversely, not as adults of God. It is this pure state before our transition into adulthood that we return to in our foundational relationship with God. No matter how old we are, He remains our Father and we remain His children.

THE STUDENT

*After three days they found him in the temple courts, sitting among
the teachers, listening to them and asking them questions.
Everyone who heard him was amazed at his understanding and his
answers. When his parents saw him, they were astonished. His mother
said to him, "Son, why have you treated us like this?"*

LUKE 2:46–50

ADOLESCENCE: 12–24[1]

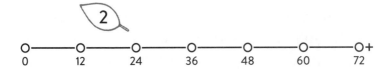

The first story depicting Jesus as a willful actor in the world is
when He is twelve years old. As curious as we might be about
the way Jesus would have been as a child (all the years before
that), it seems, as far as the canon of Scripture is concerned, unimportant. This silence is interrupted by one singular moment,

coming at what I would consider the threshold age between childhood and adolescence. (By adolescence I mean not only a time of physical transition, but one of physical, psychological, social, and neurological changes.)

It is Passover, and as was their family's custom, Jesus' parents made the annual pilgrimage to the temple in the heart of Jerusalem. Being from Galilee and from a very poor town, this would have been a remarkable moment in the life of the family and especially in the life of the adolescent Jesus. He does not only take in the sights, smells, and pageantry of this bustling place, He somehow locates and insinuates Himself into the theological conversation happening there. We find Jesus seated among the teachers and truth seekers, not just listening but contributing. This is especially significant because this young Jewish acolyte would not yet have been considered a man.

The tradition, continued to this day, was to confer adulthood on a young male at the age of thirteen. Jesus had not yet reached His bar mitzvah, and He was not just sitting among the men, but amazing them with insights of His own.

Possibly conveyed to the disciples by Jesus' mother, this story is told from the vantage point of the family who are not so much amazed by Jesus as they are annoyed. Somehow separated from the entourage as they begin the journey home to Galilee, the family eventually discovers Jesus is not with them. Exasperated, they return to find Him regaling an audience with His teachings about God. Still, the story seems less about a young savant and more about a typical teenager whose parents are exasperated by Him, however unintentionally on His part. "Everyone who heard him was amazed at his understanding and his answers. When his parents saw him, they were astonished. His mother said to Him, 'Son, why have you treated us like this?' (Luke 2:47–48). A response that now is viewed as a Christological revelation and evidence of His walking in the will of God—"Didn't you know I had to be in my Father's house?" (Luke 2:49)—might well have been received by His parents as what my grandmother called "sass."

There are a few things about this story that could be significant for our discussion. First, this is the age of Jesus in this singular story about His early life. It does seem important to know that something changed in Him at twelve. Second, it is at this point that Jesus began to act upon the world in a way that would deviate from the will and expectations of others. And finally, there was an unseen power and wisdom trapped behind the visage of an ordinary child. Even the note made by Luke was given almost as a rebuttal to the concern that He was a rebellious child: "Then he went down to Nazareth with them and was obedient to them" (Luke 2:51). Still, something has changed, and now even obedience is something Jesus must choose. Each of these are worth considering as we reflect on the common dynamics of Day 2— something all of us will be able to hold up to our own experience.

COMING OF AGE

For those of us who believe in the reality of an eternal judgment, whether that is based on the proposition of either faith or behavior, there remains the ethical conundrum around childhood and moral innocence. In other words, we will one day be judged by our actions or our faith, but surely there is a special dispensation for those who are too young to understand (and therefore be held accountable for) such things. When does a human being become old enough to be held responsible for their own choices? Biblical ethicists have called this the "age of accountability." I am not interested in entering that debate, only to offer the construct as we consider the first major transition in all of our lives: the point where we become morally aware and spiritually accountable for our own actions. I am proposing this happens around the age of twelve.

Naturally, biology plays a big part in this first transition. Puberty, which happens around this time, initiates a physical change that mirrors a more existential reality. Twelve is not a magic number; it is simply a line of demarcation between the life of a child and the emerging life of the young adult. I would argue that it is over the next twelve years where we become an adult. This Day begins and ends with two key biological markers. A process which begins with puberty and which concludes with the maturation of the brain.

We all know the radical impact of puberty, but are less aware of the massive changes our brains undergo from puberty until our early 20s. Our brains are not finished products at age twelve; they are still changing. This late neurological development explains a good bit of teenage behavior. The brain develops from bottom to top and back to front. The most primal functions of the brain are found in the amygdala at the base and back, closest to the spine. Survival, sleep, sex, and hunger are found in this small but powerful center of our emotional brain. The amygdala is also the place where both fear and aggression come from. The combination of the two and the confusing emotions they can create are part of what makes adolescent life so difficult.

The frontal lobe (the part of the brain that is farthest forward just behind the forehead) is also the last area of the brain to develop in young people. The prefrontal cortex is the portion of the brain that controls rationality, decision-making, the ability to plan; the skills that are referred to as our executive function. This is the part of the brain that helps us deal with uncertainty, generate probability, consider consequences, and generally navigate the abstract concept of time. If the amygdala is where the impulses come from, the prefrontal cortex is designed to control those impulses. Again, it is not hard to see how the late development of impulse control is a part of the adolescent challenge and a radical feature of our Day 2 development.

The adolescent years are full of social, emotional, and biological challenges. New and powerful hormones begin to course through their bodies, filling young people with almost irresistible impulses. Meanwhile, they're surrounded by equally powerful social pressures to give in to those impulses; however, the teenage brain is only beginning to master the part of the brain we need to analyze and control them. It should not be a surprise to us when adolescents are occasionally moody, insecure, or lacking in cognitive maturity. We ought to be sympathetic. When they need the executive function the most, it seems to be ineffective and unreliable. The changes are generally believed to slow and stop around twenty-four.[2] Think about that. The ability to maintain control over our internal and externalized impulses does not fully form in us until we are university graduates.

It is in this tempest of biological and sociological change that the adolescent is in what Erikson calls a "struggle for identity." Identity, the way we see and define ourselves, is formed as a generative outcome of Day 2. While every other stage transition will look to revise that identity, even creating a crisis of identity, it is only in this transition from Day 1 to Day 2 that identity is first formed.

Our physical, emotional, and social transformation culminates then in this important and invisible maturation of our brains. These are undeniably serious turning points in our biological lives and, I would argue, equally important for our spiritual lives, as our sense of self-definition can become either an anchor to Jesus in the storm of adolescence or a wedge separating us from Him.

CORE DEVELOPMENTAL CONCEPT FOR DAY 2

LEARNING

Jesus enters this season of His life asking questions, testing His ideas, and even deviating from the expectations of others. From the outside that can look like rebellion, but it is really the externalized acts of someone who is learning. Mark Zuckerberg's iconic mantra in the early years of Facebook, "Move fast and break things,"[3] is not just impetuous Silicon Valley bravado, it is a kind of manifesto for the learning mind. Whether children know it or not, it is also the mantra of the adolescent mind because this is how we really figure something out. And for the adolescent, everything is up for grabs; the whole world, including themselves, needs to be figured out.

The most important developmental concept, then, for this Day is **learning**. Adolescents are what leading neuroscience researcher Frances Jensen calls "sensation seeking learning machines."[4] The ideal conditions for this Day allow a person space to discover the world. Almost regardless of how or where we are raised, this urge to learn and to understand the world around us during this season of life is almost irrepressible. It is a time of questioning and testing the world. Having raised five teenagers so far, I have witnessed how this testing of the world can often feel destructive, but ideally it is not. Motivational speaker and author Josh Shipp uses the analogy of testing a roller coaster's lap bar.[5]

Young people pull on it not to break it, or because they want it to fail, but because they want to know if it is sturdy and will ultimately keep them safe. This testing may be perceived and received as rebellion, because this kind of experiential learning (at its rudiments) does involve trial and error. Learning is not receiving what you're being told, and it is not memorizing someone else's suppositions; true learning is experiential. It comes through triumph and failure, testing and challenging. When the teenager tells his parents he hates them, it is not a statement of fact, but an experiment in emotional honesty. Statements are really questions, hypotheses being tested. Parents would do well to remember that. It is not just a test of that idea or even of the rush of saying it, but of the parents themselves. *If I say this, will you reject me?*

Teens are testing themselves, their family, communication, conflict, love, honesty, hope, healing, and a whole wild portfolio of things, all at once.

Of course, this can be dangerous, and the real challenge for the adolescent is to test the systems they encounter without destroying them or themselves in the process. They must not pull so hard on the lap bar that they damage or even destroy it. But the pulling will necessarily involve some resistance to existing systems and assumptions. Any parent of a teenager understands this condition as something that cannot be controlled or totally repressed. On the contrary, the best way to parent a teenager is to embrace and use this drive for learning and discovery, which I believe is the adolescent's ultimate yearning. Obviously, this can be difficult on the parent, teacher, older sibling, or caregiver. Surely, each of these roles will also need to be tested. But again, this does not represent a dysfunction, but rather an expression of a healthy condition of the adolescent's identity.

IDEAL DEVELOPMENTAL CONDITION FOR DAY 2

AGENCY

As early as twelve, Jesus finds Himself at the center of the religious system of His day. And He is there to question it (Luke 2:46). Even His parents, who presumably wanted Him to leave before He was ready, find that they are also now subject to His own willful choices. In this way, Jesus is inaugurated into His own season of adolescence with a story about disappointing His parents. This is wildly significant—not just for parents, but for teenagers. In other words, we learn from this story that just because a young person does something their parents don't like does not mean they have done something wrong.

I have six kids, and I am very much aware that teenagers are often guilty of profound sin, but their attempt to assert their own autonomy is not one of them. It is both healthy and good. It is their job to rush things and the parents' job to try and slow things down; but the best parent/teenager relationship is a partnership, working together toward the child's autonomy. The ideal conditions for the development of the adolescent is ***agency***.

I choose that word because of its utility. If learning is the goal, then experimentation is essential. For the adolescent, the whole world is their laboratory. This is how they need to learn, not just by trying things but by being able to choose what they try. Think Montessori stations, not a lecture hall. Day 2 development is maximized by a growing locus of control over their own lives. Obviously, this has to be done gradually, but it is something that should begin around age twelve and culminate in what should be full emotional and faculty control by twenty-four.

Adolescents will thrive in environments where they are allowed to discover and learn, not only about the world but about themselves. They will need to make mistakes. A perfect adolescent is not a healthy adolescent. The expectation or even desire for perfection superimposed on even the most compliant teenagers will inevitably bear bad fruit, if not later in life, then in the psychological topography of their adolescence. In other words, excessive control will backfire. But equally, total permissiveness does not serve the teenager either. They will not discover their own power, their own agency, and its implications without some boundaries. We give them a laboratory equipped with walls, fire extinguishers, and clearly marked exits, and then let them experiment with whatever they want within the confines of those boundaries. Safety is not the antithesis of agency, control is.

The ideal conditions for development include the experience of increasing agency within healthy boundaries. The gains of the one and relaxing of the other should be incremental, not abrupt. If we leave the fifteen-year-old utterly on his own, to make all of his own choices, he will not experience any increase in autonomy but be overwhelmed by abandonment. However, if we refuse the fifteen-year-old any agency, operating as if he were still only a child, he will feel equally overwhelmed by the suffocation of control. Negotiating this equilibrium is surely the greatest challenge in the parent/adolescent relationship. While I do not offer any help here in how to do that, do it we must. Further, because the developmental work of Day 2 is learning, the best way to both maintain and remove boundaries is by talking through them. Even if it seems to go badly, dialogue is the currency of this unstable equilibrium. Adolescents need to be respected as both interlocutors and decision-makers. And parents will soon learn that if they will not offer room for dissent, they will lose their influence altogether.

> Safety is not the antithesis of agency, control is.

THE FINAL STAGE

It is fitting for Day 2 to culminate in an autonomous educational intensive. Heading off to university is perfectly placed for young people developmentally. Especially if that experience is somewhat away from home and requires them to take on managing their own domestic life. This transition is best done while they are still under the umbrella of learning and education. College is a wonderful option but so too is an apprenticeship, a technical course, or even something like traveling the world (what Erik Erikson called *wanderschaft*[6]). These experiences can be ideal as a kind of final project for more than a decade of experiential learning, success and failure, and identity formation.

PRIMARY DEVELOPMENTAL THREAT FOR DAY 2

INVERSION

The big threat to this Day then is what I call the sin of inversion. Testing, challenging, and exploring the nature of the world around us can lead us to the most profound and personal discoveries. But it can also lead us to the wrong conclusions about that same world.

In other words, we all collect data from the testing of the people and systems around us, but it does not mean we draw the right conclusions from that data. Sin itself becomes a critical matter on the second Day. From Day 3 onward, the major threats to our development will come from ourselves. The real threat to your growth is you. But in this adolescent Day, the biggest threat is wrapped up in the opinions and conclusions of others. The most important advice for the parents of a preteen is to pay close attention to the company they keep. The biggest influence on the development of a child is their parents, and in turn the biggest influence on the development of an adolescent is their friends. And this is a precarious proposition since the people who will most influence us in our most profound state of uncertainty are a bunch of people who are themselves also mostly lost. The overwhelming desire to begin to draw our own conclusions (which are different from our parents') is met then with the faulty conclusion of others who are themselves only testing their own metaphysical ideas.

The result is summed up by this warning from the prophet Isaiah: "Woe to those who call evil good and good evil, who put darkness for light and light for darkness, who put bitter for sweet and sweet for bitter" (Isa. 5:20). That accurately defines the sin of inversion—to see something good as evil and something evil as good; to look at the world, in our yearning for learning and discovery, and to get it exactly wrong.

Those of us who are beyond this Day can almost certainly attest to the ways we did this. The discipline of school and the boundaries set by our parents may have seemed like crimes against us in a stage when what we most wanted was freedom. The concluding thought Luke gives in the retelling of Jesus' temple episode is this: "And Jesus grew in wisdom and stature, and in favor with God and man" (Luke 2:52). This was the perfect foil to the sin of inversion. The adolescent will not be able to get everything right the first time. The key is not to imagine we can assess the world perfectly in these years, but to hold off on judgment altogether. To give our own hearts, minds, and judgment time to "grow in wisdom" as we also grow physically and build lasting relationships.

CALLING AND IDENTITY IN DAY 2

TO FOLLOW JESUS

If Day 1 and childhood offer us the non-anxious possibility that God is only asking us to be what we already are (children), so too the adolescent should not rush the deep work of being a student. What is the calling, and in turn, the formed identity for the adolescent? In the broadest possible terms, it is to be an apprentice to their own life. A big part of being a student is choosing who your teachers will be. If God is calling the adolescent to listen, try, discover, test, and learn, there is no greater partner in that journey than Jesus. The second person of the Trinity offers us this profound metaphor for the relationship between God and His people, particularly in what we perceive as the start of that relationship. It is between student and teacher, leader and follower.

At the start of His public ministry, one by one Jesus called followers to walk with Him and learn from Him. That call was also a proxy for His rule and leadership over their lives. They were being asked to give themselves wholly to Him. In this act of faith, they would find life abundant and life eternal. Likely, some, if not all, of the first twelve disciples were themselves adolescents, something we should not overlook in this discussion. Jesus could have offered those seats to older people but He didn't. Perhaps because this is the best and most critical time to decide who you will choose as rabbi in such a profound period of learning.

Even in the young disciples' calling, there is a fulfilling of their own yearning to break away from their parents. Jesus calls them not only to follow Him but to "drop their nets" and even their parents' will and control. Jesus, the master teacher, calls these young learners to Himself. He offers Himself as the solution to their yearning for identity, discovery, and even revolution.

To subordinate our newfound agency to Him is the greatest work of Day 2, to simply choose to follow Him. This then, is not just one important moment in Day 2, it is the moment by which all others are defined. And commensurate with that importance is the leadership of parents, teachers, youth workers, and caregivers to that end. Rather, than taking on the role of teacher ourselves, we ought to lead the adolescent heart toward Him.

SALVATION STARTS HERE

There are preconditions that must exist in order for the gospel to take hold of the human heart. First, and most important, is the will of God. We can't find salvation without Him, without His initiation and His propitiation. Thankfully, this condition is forever secured in the life, death, and resurrection of Jesus Christ. But that condition alone does not save us. Strangely and mysteriously, we too must play a part.

Our part, such as it is, requires the profound discovery and admission of sin and guilt in the fabric of our own lives. We have to realize our need to be saved before we can be. We are all full of sin, but sin is often devious and evades the ponderance of the human heart. So it is that we must have our own story of sin and failure, of even existential desperation in order to be able to comprehend and, in turn, apprehend the gospel. The gospel is only good news to those who have first faced the bad news of their own life choices.

Adolescence is certainly not the first time we sin, but it may be the first period of our lives in which we can comprehend our sin. More than that, it is the first time we uncover the existential tearing Paul describes in Romans 7. To know what we ought to do, even what we want to do, and to not be able to do it. Young human beings are perfectly positioned to see the grace of the gospel. They are smart enough to understand right from wrong, even to formulate a philosophical commitment to a behavior or course of action, yet they also constantly struggle with what feels like an irresistible impulse to betray that commitment. We all need a sin story to be able to hear the gospel. And adolescence is the discovery of that story.

We all need a sin story to be able to hear the gospel. And adolescence is the discovery of that story.

Sadly, the older we get the more we make peace with our sin story, declaring a convoluted truce with our inconsistencies and self-betrayals. This too uncovers the potential danger of parents who go to such great lengths to protect their teenagers from sin or error. It might seem counterintuitive (and I know it is very hard to watch), but if we do not allow our kids the room to make serious choices, they can't fail in those choices and, therefore, can't fully appreciate the grace of God. Where sin abounds grace abounds more (Rom. 5:20).

The key is to be there for our kids in that existential crisis of sin and failure. To be there waiting with the astounding good news of a God who took on human flesh to walk with them through that same pain and had that flesh pulled from His body so that they could be free. The irony of Day 2 is that we need to be allowed to get our lives horribly wrong in order for us to discover the most important truth the human heart could ever know.

TOWARD MATURITY

The English word adolescence is originally a Latin word *adolescere*,[7] which means to grow to maturity. The biblical conception of maturity is of course, not something that can be achieved by twenty-four. Yet, in a sense, the pinnacle of maturity is to finally surrender our will to His: to see and say that He is Lord and we are not. This is a lesson we will learn again and again throughout our lives, each time with new and deeper conviction. Yet, there is no comparison to this first baptism into that truth. Though it might be hard to perceive, it is very much, as Paul would say, a transition from death to life (see Rom. 6:13). And any series of events that leads us to this revelation is worth it.

If you are reading this and did not submit to the lordship of Jesus until later in your life, I would offer the old proverb about planting trees.

The best time to plant a tree is twenty years ago, and the second best time is now.

This applies to conversion as well. It may well be that the first and best time to give ourselves to Jesus is Day 2, but the second best time is whenever you finally do. Even if that is right now.

To learn from Jesus is at once the key to healthy identity formation, experiential learning, testing boundaries and false assertions, and a revolution against the broken systems we have inherited. Jesus is the perfect teacher for the developing adolescent, giving them identity, agency, and mystery. If the general call for the adolescent is to learn, then the specific call is to learn from Jesus. This one decision and an attempt at fidelity to it is the calling of Day 2.

PROCESS AND PROGRESS

I n the first six days of creation, God creates a habitat for what is to come. In other words, the elements He creates on one day make the world habitable for what comes after it. As we work through these developmental stages and the concepts that govern them, it is important to acknowledge the cumulative nature of this process. Healthy growth is not replacing one set of dynamics for another, but building on the previous discoveries. As we mature, we gain more insight, more experience, and more virtue. Each day is new in its own way, but also familiar. Growing and developing means going deeper with God and gaining greater wisdom, greater faith, greater hope, and greater love.

This is true for the skills we gain and nurture in each day of our developmental lives but also for each sense of identity. A healthy child learns that being a child is an identity imbued with grace and acceptance. As Christians, we hold on to that identity as children of God and indeed continue to understand our salvation through that identity. We do not therefore give that up when we move into Day 2 and learn to see ourselves as students. I am a child *and* I am a student. Student is just the newest sense of identity that can (and should) captivate our thoughts. But we should not lose the bonds of childhood and the profoundly important sense of play. We have those skills now, they are ours, and we ought to never let them go. Instead, it is the foundation of bonding and play that serves us as students. Then, when we move to Day 3, we learn to be servants, never ceasing to be students of life and children of God. On Day 4, we come into our own, finding real creative impact and becoming leaders. Even when we enter the second half of life, Days 5 and 6, we remain servants and lifelong learners holding on to childlike faith. We keep the lessons we learn and build on them.

This developmental ladder then is about acquisition and not just transition. We should hold on to what we have learned as our sense of who we are called to be expands. This is what developmental progress looks like. Still, the threats of each developmental Day will endanger that progress. Giving in to those temptations will produce regression from the gains of the previous Day. Progression is not guaranteed by time alone. We have to learn and grow, which means paying attention to the gift that each Day is and hearing the voice of God anew in each stage.

The final developmental Day is the culmination of all that life has taught us. The mystic knows how to play, learn, serve, create, give and leave well. They have not moved on from those rudimentary concepts but have treasured them. No matter how old we are, we do not outgrow the lessons of the previous days; we

Six Days Developmental Ladder

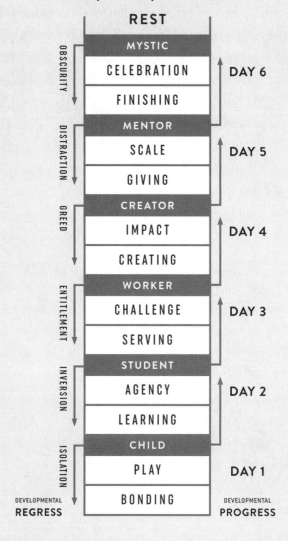

REST

| OBSCURITY | MYSTIC |
| | CELEBRATION | DAY 6
| | FINISHING |

| DISTRACTION | MENTOR |
| | SCALE | DAY 5
| | GIVING |

| GREED | CREATOR |
| | IMPACT | DAY 4
| | CREATING |

| ENTITLEMENT | WORKER |
| | CHALLENGE | DAY 3
| | SERVING |

| INVERSION | STUDENT |
| | AGENCY | DAY 2
| | LEARNING |

| ISOLATION | CHILD |
| | PLAY | DAY 1
| | BONDING |

DEVELOPMENTAL **REGRESS**   DEVELOPMENTAL **PROGRESS**

simply add to them, deepening our presence in the world. The mystic holds each of these lessons in their heart and offers them carefully to those who will listen. But even that idea, teaching others, is perhaps finally subsumed by the notion that the whole affair was one great work of preparation for the presence of God, a seventy-five-year internship for a full-time job in eternity.

DAY 3

THE WORKER

*"Then Barnabas went to Tarsus to look for Saul, and when
he found him, he brought him to Antioch."*

ACTS 11:25-26

EARLY CAREER: 24-36

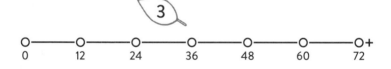

I t was Erik Erikson who first proposed that adulthood came
to us in stages (20–45, 45–65, and 65–death).[1] Still, that idea
mostly remained buried in psychoanalytical obscurity. When
most people talked about adulthood, they thought of it as any
time after childhood. In 1970, social psychologist Kenneth Keniston wrote a paper called "Youth, a New Stage of Life," in which
he argued that our 20s were a distinct developmental stage,
characterized by concepts like freedom, movement, change, and

ambivalence.² Again, Keniston's theory of a post-adolescent/pre-adulthood stage of life remained relatively unknown.

In her book *The Defining Decade*, Meg Jay argues that it was psychologist Jeffrey Jenson Arnett who would bring this concept of adolescence into the popular imagination,³ expanding on Keniston's work and offering a distinct stage of life he called "emerging adulthood."⁴ Arnett would describe a time fraught with social and economic insecurity. We have come to understand our 20s (which make up half of Day 3) as something more distinct; but still there is the cognitive temptation to define it as something that is neither childhood nor adulthood. But that is only because we tend to think of childhood and adulthood as static ideas, not developmental ones. In other words, twentysomethings are adults; they are just in a unique stage of adulthood, and doing that stage well will inevitably look different from the stages that follow it.

The first stage of adulthood is about preparing us for what comes next. If we can understand that idea, and the sovereign work of God in this time of our lives, we can begin to appreciate its features and lean in to its values.

YEARS OF PREPARATION

Like many Christians, I am fascinated by the life of the apostle Paul (also called Saul), the first apostle who was not a part of the original twelve. His story is a proxy for all of us who would come to follow Jesus (and be sent out by Him) after His resurrection. Paul is the first of our kind, called and arrested by the voice of

Jesus in a blinding light on a road, while heading somewhere else.

As much material as we have about his life, there are large portions that remain something of a mystery. Between his Road-to-Damascus conversion, his partnership with Barnabas, and eventually their ordination into missionary service in Acts 13, there are few clues as to his whereabouts and developmental journey. Somewhere between his surrender to Jesus (which would change him) and his sending into mission (which would change the world), there seems to be a time of growth and development that mirrors our own.

In the book of Galatians, Paul explains that it was fourteen years after his dramatic conversion that he went to Jerusalem. And there, his story, as told in the book of Acts, begins in earnest. Barnabas finds him there, and he brings him to a city called Antioch, presumably to help him finally accept his unique calling to the Gentiles. It is in Antioch where the elders, responding to the Holy Spirit, lay their hands on Paul and Barnabas and send them on what would be the first Gentile mission. It is not an overstatement to say that this ordination would change the world.

Still, what happens to Paul in those fourteen years between his conversion and the fulfillment of this world-altering calling? Surely, he was busy at something. It is conjecture, of course (and argument from silence), but I believe this time was anything but wasted. On the contrary, it was a developmental necessity for him. Our collective Day 3, between the ages of 24–36, can be characterized in much the same way.

Just because this is an unremarkable time (not worth adding to the Acts narrative) does not imply unimportance. On the contrary, something happened in that time which prepared Paul not only for some incredibly brave missionary work, but also for the theological revelation and spiritual maturity he would need to be worthy of such an assignment. Perhaps we all need a period of being unremarkable before we are ready to do something worthy of remark.

This is fundamental to my thesis about Day 3. In our late 20s and early 30s, we can suffer a strange cocktail of both delusions of grandeur and debilitating insecurity. We can feel we are meant to be making our mark on the world, while also feeling an increasingly desperate sense that we are not doing that at all. Both of these presumptions are usually wrong.

> **Perhaps we all need a period of being unremarkable before we are ready to do something worthy of remark.**

We don't know for sure what Paul was doing at that time, but presumably he was working through repentance for his self-righteousness and misplaced dogma. He was being discipled by people (namely Peter and Barnabas) who had known Jesus longer than he had. He was developing a theology of salvation by grace through faith. He was reconsidering the place of the law in the lives of the Gentile world. He was even doing mission, preaching the gospel to the Gentiles around him. But he was generally serving God in ways that would not be remembered. This perhaps is the most important aspect of this part of our developmental journey: to serve for a while in relative obscurity.

CORE DEVELOPMENTAL CONCEPT FOR DAY 3

SERVING

I am convinced that in the life of Paul, as in all of our lives, we must learn to follow before we can finally and fully lead. I am not like some who think of leadership as a calling for the elite. In fact, I think leadership is something that describes the confluence of two qualities: love and character. That is to say, when we become people of deep character, we will also love some unloved place or people. Driven by that love, we will want to give ourselves to those people. What is a leader if not a person we find both admirable and loving? This is the heart of spiritual leadership. It is the foundation from which we should parent and pastor, teach and mentor, supervise and start things. And in that same spirit, we are all meant to become leaders of someone, somewhere.

The path toward becoming a leader, or even just maturity itself, must pass through the land of servanthood. The work of the servant is perhaps the greatest developmental force in the world. It is sincere service that produces character and love within us. Perhaps, conversely, it is the unwillingness to serve that makes love impossible and good character elusive. Learning to lead without serving can teach us to mimic love and counterfeit character, but that kind of leadership is eventually exposed for what it is. True character can only be forged in the fires of servanthood, and true servanthood is impossible without love. We all sense we are made for something better than just serving. We all sense it because at one level it is true (Rev. 5:10). But Jesus, who was destined to rule all things, was a servant first, and it was in that breathtaking subjugation that He demonstrated His worthiness to reign. Obedience and servanthood precede exaltation. Consider this extraordinary example:

> Have the same mindset as Christ Jesus: Who, being in very nature God, did not consider equality with God something to be used to his own advantage; rather, he made himself nothing by taking the very nature of a servant, being made in human likeness. And being found in appearance as a man, he humbled himself by becoming obedient to death—even death on a cross! Therefore God exalted him to the highest place and gave him the name that is above every name, that at the name of Jesus every knee should bow, in heaven and on earth and under the earth, and every tongue acknowledge that Jesus Christ is Lord, to the glory of God the Father. (Phil. 2:6–11)

In his vulnerable and retrospective book *The Second Mountain*, David Brooks offers this correlation between character formation and service (what he calls here "giving yourself away"):

> I no longer believe that character formation is mostly an individual task, or is achieved on a person-by-person basis. I no longer believe that character building is like going to the gym: You do your exercises and you build up your honesty, courage, integrity, and grit. I now think good character is a by-product of giving yourself away. You love things that are worthy of love. You surrender to a community or cause, make promises to other people, build a thick jungle of loving attachments, lose yourself in the daily act of serving others as they lose themselves

in the daily acts of serving you. Character is a good thing to have, and there's a lot to be learned on the road to character. But there's a better thing to have—moral joy. And that serenity arrives as you come closer to embodying perfect love.

Furthermore, I no longer believe that the cultural and moral structures of our society are fine, and all we have to do is fix ourselves individually. Over the past few years, as a result of personal, national, and global events, I have become radicalized. I now think the rampant individualism of our current culture is a catastrophe. The emphasis on self—individual success, self-fulfillment, individual freedom, self-actualization— is a catastrophe. I now think that living a good life requires a much vaster transformation. It's not enough to work on your own weaknesses. The whole cultural paradigm has to shift from the mindset of hyper-in-dividualism to the relational mindset of the second mountain.[5]

Servanthood is by nature a subordinated work. This is what I mean as a developmental essential for this Day—to join something that is not yours to define or run. It is critical that we spend some time in service of someone else's vision, before we will ever be able to lead others toward our own. Because servanthood is subordination, it is hard on the ego. And in that sense it satisfies the critical Christian call to lay down our lives for others. In service, we learn to elevate the needs of others above our own. If you can't learn to deny yourself, you can't enter the kingdom (see Matt. 10:38).[6] Here is why: Serving, which is implicit self-denial, is a sacrificial gesture. We sacrifice our own agency in the service of another. And sacrifice is love embodied (see Rom. 5:6–8). We serve in order to learn to love. Servanthood then must be contrasted to slavery. Slavery is oppression precisely because it is not willingly given. Jesus does not call people to self-erasure or worthlessness. Anything that takes your agency from you, without your consent, is not servanthood; it is slavery and should be rejected. To have your autonomy taken from you is developmentally destructive. But to freely give your autonomy to another is a great act of cruciform love. Servants do not lose their autonomy; they give it as a gift. This distinction may appear subtle or even invisible to the casual observer, but it is as vast as the ocean.

In giving our service, it is important to find something that is worthy of it. That is not to say you have to find a company or organization that is perfect (even thinking that way is unhelpful), but one that is worthy—something that is doing good work or making the world better somehow. Even working at a well-run grocery store or a restaurant would qualify. They provide a real service to their customers and something that can make people's lives better. You do not have to work for a charity to see the value in the work being done.

A long period of serving will change you, and as it did Paul, potentially prepare you for something more significant. Don't rush it.

IDEAL DEVELOPMENTAL CONDITION FOR DAY 3

CHALLENGE

The simple logic of the Yerkes-Dodson Law[7] applies here.

Conceived by early twentieth-century psychologists Robert Yerkes and John Dodson, the rule reveals something especially true for Day 3. They discovered that we all have a sweet spot for performance that is related to how much or how little we are challenged. When we are underchallenged we become bored and our performance suffers, but challenge us too much, and we are overwhelmed and our performance also suffers. Somewhere in the middle, at the apex of that bell curve, is what psychologist Mihaly Csikszentmihalyi would call the flow state.[8]

Being pushed, then, to do something we are uncomfortable doing does not just accelerate learning; it facilitates a discovery of personal power, something Paul would call gifts of the Spirit (see 1 Cor. 12:1–11). Our spiritual gifts are unlocked by challenges. In terms of our early career development, this means we are most profoundly developed by being asked to do things we don't really know how to do (and possibly don't really want to do). The yearning for mastery or competence, in many ways, is the enemy of this Day's development. On Day 3, we should want to be asked to do as many kinds of tasks as possible; first, so that we can embrace the value of service and character formation as an ancillary benefit of learning that value. But second, and just as importantly, so that we can learn what we are good at. It is a bit of a treasure hunt—the results of which will be very important later in our lives.

> **We are most profoundly developed by being asked to do things we don't really know how to do (and possibly don't really want to do).**

Still, the key is to be able to try as many things as possible. The ideal Day 3 job is any job that is diverse and fraught with challenges. If a twentysomething is given the opportunity to take a job that will be ever-changing for less money than a job that is the same every day, they should take the lower pay. The money they lose will be more than made up for by the skills they gain. These kinds of jobs can seem frustrating since a person may always be feeling like a novice. But it is exactly that feeling that is the great gift of Day 3. The amateur learns through love. It is exactly this varied experience that will, in time, teach us what it is we most love to do.

MY STORY

Straight out of college, I was offered a ministry position with InterVarsity Christian Fellowship. I was asked to plant a fellowship at a major university where they had no presence. Right out of college, I was expected to be able to:

1. Write compelling updates
2. Preach and speak publicly
3. Study and teach the Bible
4. Develop training curriculum
5. Create strategic plans
6. Lead small groups
7. Disciple one-to-one
8. Counsel students
9. Lead teams
10. Organize conferences

11. Handle chapter accounting
12. Manage data
13. Serve as a liaison with the university
14. Relate to and socialize with students
15. Raise money
16. Cultivate strong trusting relationships with donors
17. Organize a local advisory board
18. Manage my own time to do all of this
19. Stay culturally relevant and intellectually sharp

No one can be good at all of those things. And that is the point. This kind of job was perfect for Day 3 exactly because it asked so much from someone so unqualified. Very early on I discovered which parts of the job I liked and was more disposed to and which parts were a struggle. And while I might have enjoyed the preaching and struggled with writing annual budgets, I learned how to serve by doing them all. It is too soon in our character development to decide which things we will and will not do. If we rush that, we will not learn the deeper personal lesson that every leader must learn: how to follow and how to serve.

But it is also too soon for our skill development. While there will be roles that we immediately take to, and some we find distasteful, we can't know for sure where our gifts lie until we have persevered through that initial experience. I was not naturally drawn to administration or financial responsibility, but, in time, I became competent and came to rely deeply on those skills in the service of my more obvious gifts. Some skills bring less immediate reward or accolades, and so we can miss an area where we are gifted simply because we have not done it enough to see just how important it is. Being asked to do so many different kinds of tasks was a profound gift to me, but it was only through persevering in those tasks that I was able to discover my long-term gifts and competencies.

We want to be asked to do as many different kinds of tasks as possible and in turn asked to push through the initial feelings of incompetence in order to find out just where we can really shine. This is a longer process than we think.

Robert Clinton, in his wonderful material on Life Long Leadership, has argued that there are three big questions that govern the developmental journey of our lives. He says the key question at this stage of our lives is the question "Who am I?" For context, that question eventually gives way to the second and third questions, "What is my contribution?" and "What will my legacy be?"[9] We are often tempted to rush the first question to get to the second. Twenty-five-year-olds can often feel a strong and unnatural pressure to be able to answer the second question before they have really been given time to answer the first. I like Clinton's first question for Day 3 because it places identity squarely in the middle of a decade of doing. We should be hard at work in our late 20s and early 30s, trying, succeeding, failing, and learning about ourselves through the experience of work and commitment. It is on Day 3 that we earn what sociologist James Côté calls "identity capital."[10]

Incidentally, this is one way that our graduation from university with a specific degree can be psychologically counterproductive. Despite the implication of "majoring" in the degree seeking process, we do not need to know what our contribution to the world will be when we are twenty-two years old; not even really when we are thirty. On the contrary, this is exactly the time to be answering the more relevant question of identity (who am I?), which will lead us to clarity on the question of contribution. This is why we are best advised to learn to serve on Day 3 and try our hand at as many things as possible. These two commitments will reveal where we are uniquely ready to make our mark on the world.

If you are in Day 3, don't rush the first question to get to the second. It is in the place of serving someone else that we discover both what we are good at and what we are made of.

PRIMARY DEVELOPMENTAL THREAT FOR DAY 3

ENTITLEMENT AND IMPATIENCE

All of this may seem self-evident, even desirable to the twentysomething person. I have not talked to many people who would dismiss these ideas out of hand. The pushback comes when we are talking about twelve years. Learning to serve, even trying new things, surely can be accomplished in less time, right? So it is that patience is vital to our development in a time when patience is not seen as a primary virtue. Research done by Anders Ericsson and popularized by Malcom Gladwell has given us the 10,000-hour rule.[11] Mastery is not achieved through natural talent but hard work . . . and a lot of it. Rationally, we understand that we will not be great at any one thing until we have had lots of time for what Ericsson called "deliberate practice."[12] That is, doing it with the intention of improving.

The sin that creeps into Day 3 for all of us is not so much that we want to rush to mastery before we are ready but that we believe we should not have to put in that kind of time. This sin can manifest from the inside, as the belief that others may need a decade to learn to be a servant, but "I sure won't." Or from the outside: the pressure of unrealistic expectations of others to have achieved something world-changing right out of college.

The archetypal tech hero that drops out of college, certain of the mark they will make on the world, is not only modern mythology, it is the exception that proves the rule. In other words, these are not fully true stories to start with, and even if they are, it is their rarity that makes them noteworthy, proving that this is not how most of us should expect our lives to unfold.

Today, twentysomethings are expected to have arrived, and that expectation is both unfair and unhealthy. The end result, and what I would consider the biggest threat to this season of life, is entitlement. There is a strong temptation to feel entitled to a job with no disagreeable tasks. We can feel entitled to only do jobs we enjoy, only work with people we like, and only receive feedback that is positive. We can feel entitled to the fruit of mastery without the long hard work of achieving it. We can feel entitled to the respect of leadership without having given that same respect (over a long period of time) to anyone ourselves.

We can feel entitled to success, compensation, prominence, and power before we have done the hard work to earn it. This entitlement threatens our development precisely because those may well be things that God has in store for us, but just not yet. But by demanding them before we have really earned them, we undermine what will be a more grounded and even humble version of those rewards.

It is perhaps significant then that so many of us will get married during Day 3. The vast majority of Americans will marry before the age of thirty, with the median age for first marriage being twenty-six and twenty-eight for women and men, respectively.[13] This might seem like a contradiction (or even a mistake) since we are still just trying to figure out who we are. Knowing so little about what we really like (and don't like) seems like a recipe for disaster for marriage. And certainly for some it is. Yet, I think that has as much to do with a misunderstanding of marriage as it does with our incomplete sense of self.

You see, marriage is really more about *mutual* submission (which is another way of describing love) than about compatibility. Often marriages will work not because two people are perfectly suited but because two people learn to love, respect, and accept each other. This hard work of mutual submission is perfect for Day 3. In other words, we are already meant to be learning to let go of our ego and our spoiled notions of entitlement anyway. In that sense, marriage is the perfect addition to the work of Day 3. Still, marriages often fail for the same reason our Day 3 development fails: impatience.

Sometimes referred to as the "seven-year itch," something happens to marriages about seven years in. We all enter into marriage with selfish intentions, but marriage, we discover, only works if we can die to ourselves and truly love another person. It seems the shelf life for selfish love is about seven years. This is not just a modern phenomenon. The median duration of a marriage in 1922 was 6.6 years; in 1974, 6.5 years[14]; and in 1990, 7.2 years.[15] The exact Day this disillusionment happens is less important than that it does happen, to everyone. We all hit a wall and wonder if this is what we really want. We all are tempted to look for something else. And if the average person is married in their mid- to late 20s, then they will also experience this seven-year wall by the end of Day 3. The marriages that survive are often transformed into something deeper and more substantial. I would argue this is because they have learned the important lessons that God was teaching us on Day 3: to serve, to submit, and to learn to be patient.

CALLING AND IDENTITY IN DAY 3

WORKER/TEAMMATE

There is a moment in the life of every disciple that is both thrilling and terrifying. When Jesus called His first young followers, He called them to serve His cause, to learn obedience, and to try a million new things. That call to follow Him involved a surrendering of their will, plans, and vision for the future. They laid all that down to walk with Him. The initial invitation must have felt (as it does for all of us) like one part sacrifice and one part privilege. And so it is. Yet, over time they may have become comfortable with the arrangement as they experienced the grace of good leadership. It is nice to just do what you are told and to be free from having to make certain decisions, especially when you know the person leading knows what they are doing.

But perhaps even more thrilling and terrifying is that moment when Jesus tells them they will need to walk on without Him. Or at least without Him in the same way they were used to. Now they would have to step into what Søren Kierkegaard called the "dizziness of freedom."[16] And while Jesus promised His Spirit would be right there with them, as it is with all believers, His Spirit would also not command them, nor us. This fascinating transition from disciple to apostle, from follower to leader, from student to teacher, and from apprentice to maker helps us understand both sides of the transition a bit better.

To know, for instance, that eventually it will be our turn to take the lead can make it easier to be a follower. By knowing what is to come on Day 4, the calling of Day 3 begins to make more sense. Further, the temptation to rush that development, to be impatient for our chance to call the shots, becomes especially problematic. The calling of Day 3 is to work. But that is too limited in scope. What I really mean is teamwork. I would use the term "teamworker," if it weren't so awkward, to best define being a part of something you are not leading. Being a teamworker, such as in a highly ordered context like the military, means to be a good soldier who can follow orders and trust that the people moving the pieces know what they are doing (or at least that they are the ones who are responsible for that).

The call of God on those of us in Day 3 is to serve the team. In doing so, we learn the invaluable lessons of character, which are unlearnable without submission. Further, our willingness to do anything that is needed results in a flurry of skill acquisition unmatched in any other time in our lives. It is on this day that the healthy soul discovers that Jesus was right—when we lay down our lives, we find them. In the willing gift of our agency (which we discover on Day 2), we find ourselves. We lay down our will to find out who we really are. From that place of submission, we become worthy to be submitted to. Skipping this step, as we have all seen, can produce demagogues who want to be followed and obeyed even though they themselves have never wholeheartedly followed or submitted to anyone themselves.

Day 3 is still about answering the burning (and still unanswered) questions of identity. How has God gifted me? What kind of work brings me joy? What kind of work unnaturally drains me? Where do I see that something in the world really needs to change? Because I have walked in the world for a while, where am I beginning to see that I might be able to do things better? These questions build upon themselves, consummating in Day 4.

TRANSITIONS, THE NIGHTTIME OF DECISION

Using the six days of creation as a rubric for the creative work of God in and through the course of our lives is probably most helpful in the light of day. That is, for the majority of our lives, we will be doing what we think we are supposed to be doing without giving much thought to it. But there are also moments when we are not sure about anything. You may have picked up this book because you are in just such a moment.

And there are such moments in the margins of that first creation story. In between the lucid work of God to create life is the hidden silence of night. A refrain that echoes through every day is, "And there was evening, and there was morning"—the first day, the second day, the third day . . .

If the work of creation is filled with light and life, then the silence of nighttime is filled with darkness and doubt. This too is a part of the journey, and we must pass through the night of each day in order to find the morning again. Of course, I mean this metaphorically. But in many ways, these night experiences are as real as they are hard. They could very well be filled with sin, betrayal, failure, and literal death, and the grief and pain that accompany them all. But whatever shape it takes, the night is proxy for unknowing. In between the brightness of clarity and calling, there are short seasons of uncertainty, confusion, and even existential lostness. It can creep up on us or hit us like a bus. Sometimes attached to a jarring event, our greatest suffering can also be a catalyst for transition.

As I write this, here are some of the things I have witnessed the people in my sphere going through in just the last two weeks:

- A diagnosis of cancer
- The sudden loss of a child. And then a second one
- The inexplicable betrayal of a best friend
- The shame of public sin
- Divorce
- Being fired from a job that defined you
- Being told by your adolescent child that they hate you
- A dream that dies
- Plans that fail
- Friends who don't show up when you need them most
- A dying prayer life
- Cynicism taking over your heart
- Waking up one day and realizing your life is nothing like you thought it would be. A feeling of futility, that you have accomplished nothing

While each experience is unique, the feeling of desolation is common to us all. Rest assured these experiences and the emotions that accompany them are both normal and unavoidable. Not easy, but normal. They can be as mild as a sense that what we are doing just isn't working anymore and that it is time for something new, something we have not figured out yet. And they can be as extreme as what the fifteenth-century Cistercian monk John of the Cross called his "dark night of the soul"[1] and what Ignatius called "times of desolation."[2] Something between an unsettled feeling and a true emotional crisis tends to accompany each of these transitions from one day to another. Of course, I'm positing that these developmental Days last for a dozen years, so the night will come only a few times in our lives. Such night time experiences shouldn't be happening to us more frequently than that. If we can't find our way through them, or they never seem to abate, then we are talking about something else. Anything more chronic and you should look for other explanations and possibly seek help.

But, in the course of a normal developmental pattern, you will hit more than one wall. You will find yourself asking those identity questions precisely because your identity is supposed to change. The night is ultimately a severe but priceless gift.

It is in the night that we rethink things. It is in the night that we reconsider the way things are, which makes a new way possible. As you come to the end of one of these psychosocial development stages, you will probably not pass seamlessly into the next stage. Instead, you will likely experience some internal resistance to the new calling. But at the same time you may feel that something needs to change.

The best way through that resistance is to acknowledge what is happening and welcome that still small voice of God initiating some change in you. That the sense of instability and uncertainty is both normal and healthy and even necessary for the next day to dawn. Between evening and morning is the struggle of the night; you can't really skip it.

Next, you should turn your face toward Jesus, and not just because He has the answers but because He knows what you are feeling. He has been there too, and He was perfect.

Jesus was betrayed. In perfection, He was still the victim of betrayal.

Jesus was discouraged. In perfection, He still lost heart at the half-heartedness of the people around Him.

Jesus considered quitting. In perfection, He still asked God for a way out.

Jesus was murdered by the people He was trying to love and save. In perfection, His leadership was still not enough to convince them.

You know that, but here is the part you may not know. This ravaged Jesus emotionally. He had moments of emotional crisis and wreckage. And in those moments, those dark nights, He sought consolation and renewed calling in the company of friends and in the presence of His Father.

He took Peter, James, and John along with Him, and He began to be deeply distressed and troubled. "'My soul is overwhelmed with sorrow to the point of death,' he said to them. 'Stay here and keep watch'" (Mark 14:34).

So, turn to Jesus because only He can offer you both consolation and direction. You turn to Jesus because He knows, He sees, and He is ready to lead you. Again, this calling cycle starts with crisis but can, and should, drive us to intimacy. Intimacy—time in the presence of God—will then lead us to a renewed (if slightly changed) identity and calling. Night will give way to a new day.

Blaise Pascal died in 1662. Sometime after his death, a housekeeper found a handwritten note sewn into the lining of his coat. It was a journal entry of sorts from what he called his "night of fire."

A turning point, this night recounts an encounter with God. Pascal wrote: "FIRE. GOD of Abraham, GOD of Isaac, GOD of Jacob not of the philosophers and of the learned. Certitude. Certitude. Feeling. Joy. Peace." What starts with fire ends with peace. So, too, is our hope for the nighttime of the transitions we will face.

THE MAKER

"The unexamined life is not worth living."

SOCRATES[1]

"The unlived life is not worth examining."

SHELDON KOPP[2]

MID CAREER: 36–48

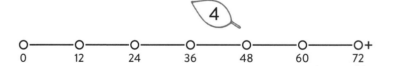

A t some level we all hope to live well, or do something with our lives that matters, that will be remembered or make the world a better place somehow. I simply do not know of any way to discern such a path, or for that matter, how to assess such a thing without God's input. If each of us is able to accomplish something special with the one life we have been given, to cre-

> Someone says "I have found my calling" as a way of describing a job that seems to fit them perfectly. . . . This way of thinking about calling is essentially atheistic.

ate something beautiful, it stands to reason that the God who created us would know how best to do that. This is why the notion of calling (however it is labeled) is so important. We sense this potential in our lives precisely because it is real. Our lives are meant to create something unique that makes the world better somehow.

In popular parlance, the idea of calling has something to do with excellence and/or a kind of compulsion to work in a certain field. Someone says "I have found my calling" as a way of describing a job that seems to fit them perfectly. That sentiment creates a certain pressure on everyone else to find that same sense of job satisfaction in their career. This way of thinking about calling is essentially atheistic. That is to say we can integrate the notion of calling without a personal God who is doing the calling. It also attaches the experience of calling to fulfillment. And while I do agree that to follow the will and leading of God for your life will ultimately fulfill you, there is a strong biblical case to be made that it will not always immediately do so. It is more plausible to expect that God will call us to things that are both difficult and unpleasant in the short term. At the height of Jesus' own ministry and calling, He found Himself increasingly opposed by His enemies, misunderstood by His followers, and even betrayed by His friends.

In one of the most tender, raw, and vulnerable episodes of Jesus' life, we witness His terror at facing the prospect of the

Father's call on His life. In the garden of Gethsemane, He travails to accept the cup of suffering that is, in fact, the will of God for Him. He is being called to die. Not only to die, but die alone, isolated by ignorance, accusation, and dishonor. This was not the Father's ultimate will for Him, for we also know the call on His life was to die *and* to rise. To die in order to redeem and renew all things. To die in order to reign in power. But that initial step of suffering was not easy to swallow, and Jesus revealed an honest reticence to accept it. Perhaps the fate of the whole world is won in the faith-filled resignation of Jesus, when He finally and bravely concedes, "Yet not what I will, but what you will" (Mark 14:36).

So it is that we are not well-served by thinking about calling as a synonym for personal or professional fulfillment. There will be times when what we are called to do is so difficult that we find it depleting. This is not necessarily a sign that we are doing the wrong thing. As we have already explored in Day 3, a good part of the calling of our 20s is to do just that. To endure certain tasks because we know that there is more to life than job satisfaction, namely character and self-discovery. It is precisely in the work we dislike that we grow in the foundational virtue of servanthood while also uncovering our gifts. But what happens once those two gifts have been sufficiently received? When we have in fact learned to follow, to serve, and to do some dirty work? What happens once we have begun to identify the things we do especially well and the other things we do consistently poorly? If these revelations are indeed part of the goal and calling of God on our lives in that stage of life, what is the result?

THE ADVENTURE WE ARE READY FOR

Famed professor of literature Joseph Campbell, in his landmark work *The Hero with a Thousand Faces,* achieved something extraordinary by comparing mythology (important stories told by societies) across culture and time. The hero, he discovered, has a common, predictable journey. In other words, all of our stories seem to reveal either a common experience or at least a common yearning. In an interview with Bill Moyers, Campbell, remarking on this "hero's journey," began to muse on the idea of serendipity. Sometimes the journey of the hero just comes to him on the road he's already on.

As someone who is growing in my understanding and appreciation of the sovereignty of God, I found this conversation sparkling with insight. Campbell would go on to say, "The achievement of the hero is the one that he is ready for, and is really a manifestation of his character. And it's amusing the way in which the landscape and the conditions of the environment match the readiness of the hero. The adventure that he is ready for is the one that he gets."[3] Campbell's insights, whether he knows it or not, are deeply Christological; and Jesus, the archetype of all heroic stories, waited thirty years before entering public ministry. If He needed time to prepare, surely, we do too.

So it is that the preparation and character formation of Day 3 plays a vital role in the adventure and even achievement of Day 4. It is indeed sometimes amusing to see the way in which the landscape of our lives suddenly opens up with opportunities that seemed to elude us only a few years earlier. But these "opportunities" do seem to match the readiness of the called person. If you have not prepared yourself for them, they do not emerge. Instead, what seems like a lucky break is really a beautiful combination of grace and reward, derived from obedience to God, servanthood, and character development. The adventure you are ready for is the one you get.

This is the wonder of Day 4. While we may have been dissatisfied with incompatible job assignments in our early 20s because of impatience, in our early 30s we begin to feel the same dissatisfaction but for a very different reason. We feel it now because it is time for a change. That change could be something as narrow as the job we are doing, or it could be as broad as the organizations we participate in. It is in this season of life that systems can and should be challenged; that new ideas, new approaches and even new organizations will emerge. For the most disaffected, this may well be the time to break away from the institutions under which you have served in order to forge a new form or blaze a new trail. For others, it just might look like finding a more fitting job within the systems we find ourselves. And for those in highly restrictive professional environments, it could look like a feeling of stagnation in our life patterns or even social circles. On this Day, we know ourselves well enough to be able to say: This is what I do well, and this is what I do poorly. This is what motivates me; this is where you will get the best from me. And conversely, this is what drains me and where I find my productivity and morale will be at its lowest.

This is the time in our lives and career where we look for jobs and roles that fit our strengths and where we will be able to allow those strengths to flourish. This is not to say that we never serve again, or that we take jobs with no unpleasant aspects. But it does mean that we find some focus so that we can take these critical years of our lives and make a real contribution. This is the Day we are meant to make a lasting mark on the world. In many ways, it is the apex of our life's journey and the gift of work we will give to the world. I want to call this focusing movement the work of creation.

CORE DEVELOPMENTAL CONCEPT FOR DAY 4

MAKING/CREATING

Every life is an act of creation. For that reason, every life is a work of art. And this is never more apparent than in Day 4. In this season of life, the primary work is creating. Building on the foundation of Day 3, a person now has enough information about themselves, their skills, motivations, and gifts to be able to ask and answer the deepest questions of calling: What is something that only I am able to create and offer to the world? What unique thing can I do, start, or plant? The ideal conditions for this Day, therefore, afford us the agency to usher in some kind of change and its corresponding impact. In some ways, this could be the climax of our work life. The catalyst for this Day, as in the ones before and after, is some kind of identity crisis, or what Erikson called "role confusion."[4] We find ourselves discontented with the status quo of our lives, and in turn, unhappy with the role we play in it. It is from the fires of that discontentment that we are meant to create something new.

MY STORY

As I have already shared, for the first ten years of my career, I worked for a collegiate parachurch ministry trying, failing, and learning from a diverse palette of skills and experiences, but not only that, learning to submit to the vision of an organization I did not start or run. I learned to be supervised and to follow the leadership and direction of regional and national leaders, as well as submit to the corporate decision-making of a team. At the end of that season, I found myself full of clarity about myself (what I was good and not so good at) and about the world I was inhabiting. For me there was a disconnect between the church and the parachurch that was less than ideal, at best, and unbiblical at worst. This critical view coupled with some experience, not only in mission, but in leadership, gave me a platform from which to launch innovative change.

It is possible to take our frustrations and ideas of how things might be done better and simply bury them. We can do that by only talking about the problem; we can do that by ceasing to talk about the problem. But it is also possible to take our ideas about how things ought to be out of the shadows of critique and into the daylight of creation. Not that I am somehow the example of all these things, that is my point: I am not special. This is how we all should be thinking in our early to mid-30s. I took the next twelve years to dream, plant, iterate, and cultivate the missional experiment that is the UNDERGROUND Network.[5] It was my act of Day 4 creation.

In many ways Day 4 is the apex of our calling. It is the summit of our working lives. We are meant to take all of that experience, character, and clarity about ourselves into the realm of the artist. We are meant to make something. For many of us it will not be related to our job at all. Not everyone can follow this developmental journey in the stages of their career. But remember, we are talking about calling, the growing evolution of the voice of God calling us into His mission at each distinct phase of our lives. Your calling, in that sense, is so much bigger than your job. For most of us, our jobs will allow us some access or opportunity to fulfill that calling to create in Day 4. But even those of us who find and labor in "ministry" jobs, there will always be aspects of that work that are utilitarian and outside our core calling. That is not a problem. You can think of your calling to create something as an overlapping circle with your job. For some, the circles overlap almost entirely; for others, they may barely overlap at all. But just as surely as you have employment (a place you try to make a living), so too you have the second circle (a place you try to make the kingdom come).

JOB

CREATIVE CALLING

A place you try
to make a living

A place you try to make
the kingdom come

The key developmental concept then, for Day 4, is creation. You are meant to make something, to offer something to the world that was not there before. You are meant to do, write, start, plant, establish, or otherwise make something that only you can make. It is not that you will make something that has never been made before, but something that could not be made if you were not alive and saying yes to God. So much of that equation has to do with the unique contours of who you are. To make something you first have to realize that you are utterly unique. What makes us all the same is that we all experience the yearning at this point in our lives to make a mark, to leave the world somehow changed by our having been there. But what makes us different is the way we respond to that. A seasoned nurse finds a new process for patient care that heals more than the body; a teacher writes a one-of-a-kind curriculum for her one-of-a-kind context; an athlete starts a training program for kids who come from his neighborhood; a mother starts a group for mothers where she can pass on what she has learned; a longtime church member starts a microchurch in her home. What you make may have been done before, but never by you and never in your particular way.[6]

IDEAL DEVELOPMENTAL CONDITION FOR DAY 4

IMPACT

It is not that we abandon servanthood in Day 4. As I have mentioned, servanthood, like childhood, is a posture we never lose. But the servant is essentially reactive, asking the question "How can I help?" and then finding a way to help, even if there is a disconnect between what is needed and our ability to meet that need. In Day 4, we move from that posture as essential and feel empowered by God to do something proactive. After gaining a perspective that has probably been growing for years, we see a problem and feel a strong compulsion to find a way to fix it. This is an urge to make an impact, and being in an environment where that is possible is the ideal developmental condition for Day 4. It is an urge that would have been building all through Day 3. It is not that we only start to dream of impact in Day 4; in many ways we yearn for it all our lives. But it is in this season that we are best equipped to achieve it. If, in Day 2, we were asking of our environment, "What is there to learn here?" and in Day 3, "How can I serve?" then in Day 4 we are asking "Where will I have the greatest impact?" It may well be that you have more than one creative impulse on this Day. Perhaps you should pursue them all, but you will have the greatest sense of fulfillment in the place of greatest impact.

As with every transition between Days, the shift from servant-focused leadership to what almost can feel like self-serving leadership can make the head spin. We might be tempted to see the invitation to break away and create as a temptation or a regression in character. But this too is a part of the maturity we should gain from more than a decade of serving and following. It is not selfish to give the art of your life away; it is selfish not to. As much as we were willing to be supportive and even unseen up to this point, we now must be willing to step up and step out, to take a risk and do something that has not been done before, to assert ourselves, our vision of the world, in some small way, and in turn somehow change it.

PRIMARY DEVELOPMENTAL THREAT FOR DAY 4

GREED

There is a notion that has been set loose in the Western Christian world that the Bible serves as a kind of guidebook, and when properly applied, the result is a superlative life. In other words, if you do it right, you will be healthy, wealthy, and wise. More than that, you will have godly children, a fireproof marriage, incorruptible friends, and somehow avoid pesky human problems like mental illness, addiction, and cancer. Of course, this is not at all what the Bible teaches about itself, or more to the point, about the role of the words of God in our lives. In many ways, the presence of the living and active Word of God (another way of talking about calling) is to cut us, challenge us, and generally reveal our hearts as desperate. The best thing about God's Word is that it draws us closer to Him. It does not promise us deeper communion with idols and the counterfeit gods of our context: it offers us deeper communion with Jesus and His creative work through us.

> God's Word does not promise us deeper communion with idols and the counterfeit gods of our context: it offers us deeper communion with Jesus and His creative work through us.

Still, we are forever fighting that fight to draw close to Jesus and not trade that intimacy for a worldly substitute. You might think that the temptations of Day 3 are the most formidable, but it is Day 4 that holds the greatest danger in this regard. Faith in youth is full of fire and commitment. It is exactly because Jesus beckons us to come and die, to give up everything to follow Him, that the twentysomething psyche wants to say yes. We are in our right minds to be drawn to the sheer magnitude of it all. The King and His kingdom come to us through total surrender, not compromise and capitulation. I had a friend who used to say: it is for the young to fight the devil. And so they know it, but the devil waits for us. And for those who made strong commitments in their 20s—who made sacrifices for their faith, who found both community and intimacy in that life—the creative potential of Day 4 is suddenly threatened by radical commitment fatigue.

It is fine to give away most of your money to the poor when all your friends are broke. It is fine to share a house with other believers in your 20s. It's edgy, even cool to share. It is fine to boldly proclaim Jesus at work when you can easily find another job that pays the same. It is fine to drive an old car, to give the keys to anyone who asks to borrow it. It seems easier to live on less and love without limit. But try that when you are forty-two and see how you feel. The call to lay down our lives is never more under threat than in Day 4 precisely because we are at the zenith of our creative calling. The devil will find new interest in you as you stand on the precipice of creating something unique and beautiful for the kingdom and in Jesus' name. At that moment, you can expect to also be simultaneously tempted by all the shiny things that surround you.

Christians in their 40s suddenly find themselves surrounded by peers at the height of their earning potential. Living with other people? Driving an old car? Choosing to be out of fashion? You thought high school was hard? That is superficial compared to the threat of greed in Day 4. The life of surrender to Jesus will almost certainly mean you will *not* have the best house on the block. That you will feel behind the promotional advancement of your colleagues and friends. Even if you were called to climb that ladder, you are not called to spend the spoils in the same way that the world does. The sacrifices of Day 3, which seemed grounded and radical, might now feel irresponsible. But they are not. Do not let the profoundly alluring siren song of greed grip your heart, which, in my experience, can easily happen in Day 4. If you do, it will certainly cost you as a creator, just as the best artists are often poor, not because poverty generates hunger, but because being in need leads them to make the right kind of art. It speaks to the desperate.

CALLING AND IDENTITY IN DAY 4

MAKER

The first and greatest story of creation is the story of God. Our Father was the first maker. The cosmos itself begins with sound and light. It has always been a wonder to me that secular scientists' best theory for the beginning of the world is called the "big bang," another way of saying a single photoacoustic event from which the universe expands. And in those first lines of our ancient text, we are told that God said, "Let there be light." Into the nothing He SPEAKS, and LIGHT explodes the cosmos into existence. Sound and light. Maybe He has never stopped doing that. We have the world because He spoke and His word illuminates everything else. Each transition is like that for us—a visitation of that ancient memory to hear Him say a word to us, to shine a light on one thing from a chaotic sea of possibilities.

Yet, that was just the beginning of His creative work. The Maker was making a world for us, each layer being laid for the final creation that would most closely resemble Him. He was not just making a world, He was making a family. He makes a world so that a family can emerge and live in it. This has both beautiful and breathtaking implications for us.

> **Each transition is like that for us—a visitation of that ancient memory to hear Him say a word to us, to shine a light on one thing from a chaotic sea of possibilities.**

For Erikson, the real threat to adulthood was found in the tension between intimacy and isolation. We are pulled between the dueling urges to form deep and lasting relationships or to withdraw into isolation. If we overlay that concern on the idea of creation and greed we can see the same tension. For most of us, this season of life will find its deepest meaning when we are making something for the world. But we are never called to do that alone. In this work of creation, we will also find coconspirators who become dear and lasting friends. If, on the other hand, we choose to be distracted and dazzled by the lesser lights of the world, we will instead find ourselves more isolated and alone.

If forced to choose between a job that allows you to create something or a job that pays you better, the choice is clear. The pay may give you better things but not better relationships. And as we will all eventually discover (usually at the end of our lives) relationships are the only real wealth we ever acquire. I am not saying that money is unimportant, only that it is a weak substitute for the community that creation can create. The act of starting something, for instance, will also mean a new series of deeply meaningful friendships with people who rally around the thing you are called to create. The call to make something is also an initiation into a community because you are probably not the only person God is calling.

Answering the question about what you will make with your life is an invitation into a family of people who are also called to make the same thing with their lives. And of course, our art is also mission so it is also meant to relieve and redeem people in need. I do not know exactly what you will be called to make in this Day, but I know you will not be called to make it alone, and I know that the people served by it will also form a community.

The identity of Day 4, then, is one of artist, maker. But, the art we make is not only for us, it is meant to somehow recall the first archetype of creation. To hear the Word of God call us into the work of co-creation, to make something that was not there before and to see a new community form around it.

THE PRAYER OF INDIFFERENCE

The key to hearing God is indifference. This idea comes from Ignatius of Loyola and has seen a recent revival by neo-Ignatian proponents like Ruth Haley Barton. She writes:

> There are, in fact, two aspects of this prayer. There is the prayer *for* indifference in which we open to the gift by asking for something we do not yet have. And then there is the prayer *of* indifference which is the answer to that prayer—the ability to say, in truth, "I am indifferent to anything but the will of God." The prayer *of* indifference carries us across the threshold between two worlds—from the world of human will and action to a world in which we are participants in the Divine will that has already been set in motion.[1]

In one sense, all spiritual decisions are a journey "across the threshold between two worlds," but especially those related to developmental transitions in our calling. The prayer of indifference, and the struggle to pray it, is most perfectly embodied by Jesus in the garden before His arrest. "'Abba, Father,' he said, 'everything is possible for you. Take this cup from me. Yet not what I will, but what you will'" (Mark 14:36).

Not what I will. But what You will.

Indifference toward your own will, coupled with passionate commitment to His—this is the key to discerning the voice of God.

We like the idea of hearing God and believe at some principled level that it is possible, but for many of us it never seems to happen. Christian people seem to fit into two extreme categories, those who think they hear God speak to them word for word about what detergent to buy and those who don't know of a single clear word they have ever received. Most of us are in the middle and maybe leaning toward the wordless side.

> **Indifference toward your own will, coupled with passionate commitment to His—this is the key to discerning the voice of God.**

Underneath this whole discussion of calling, lifelong development, transitions, and identity is the implicit assertion that God is speaking in a way that we can and should be able to hear. I am convinced that God does routinely speak to us in ways that we can both hear and understand. Behind all theology of revelation is the idea that God will only be known if He wants to be. And all evidence points to His desire for us to know Him, His self-revelation holds the world together. And yet, we struggle so much to discern His voice. If I am right and He is speaking, then the issue is either noise (we can't hear Him over the din around us) or it is language (we do not understand the constructs of the language He is using). In both cases, the fault does not lie with God, who we imagine to be silent, but in the listener who is distracted by other things or confounded by the sound of His voice.

The real issue is competing voices. We may sense/hear God say something to us, about say our future, but then we immediately hear several other voices in our head competing for prominence and confusing the first word. We hear the voice of the controlling people in our lives, immediately imagining what they would say about the decision, thought, or course of action. We hear the voice of our own selfish desires. We hear the voice of our bad theology denying the gentle word as too easy and the challenging word as too harsh. And perhaps more than anything, we hear the voice of our idols, whatever they may be. These false gods make counterdemands to undermine the claim that God has on our hearts, wills, and lives. As soon as God says go, the idol says stay. As soon as God says give, the idol says hold. As soon as God says lay it down, the idol says double down. And there, right at the epicenter of our prayer life and our decision-making, is the struggle of the Christian life, the struggle to make and keep Jesus Lord. He is asking for our allegiance and obedience, but so are our idols. Money, greed, fame, position, desirability, popularity, lust, control, self-determination . . . all of these want to be god instead.

The real work of prayer then is to silence those voices. To take from our idols the right to own us, to lead us and to command our hearts. The real work of hearing God then is not in straining to listen, but in surrender to the one who is speaking. This is why the key to hearing God is indifference. And the key to indifference is worship. For me, hearing God is easy; it is laying down my life that is hard. Instead of closing our eyes, asking a question, and then listening for an answer, we ought to set aside time for worship. Lots of time. As much time as it takes to get to the place of indifference to the voices of idols, to the place of total surrender. That is worship after all.

If you need to hear God on something, read through the Psalms, shut the door, and put on music and sing until your heart and mind are captured completely by the love of God in the face of Christ Jesus. The longer you worship, the clearer your world will become. Worship until you can say with certainty: *Nothing matters to me more than You. Bid me and I will go anywhere, do any service to the end of the earth.* Feel the liberation that submission brings. Lay to rest your idols by making Jesus utterly Lord. Then when you raise the one matter before you, there will be no barriers to hearing Him. A faithful heart can be trusted. What you hear in that moment, when you are truly indifferent to the answer, you can trust.

DAY 5

THE MENTOR

*"Even if you had ten thousand guardians in Christ,
you do not have many fathers."*

1 COR. 4:15

"She did what she could."

MARK 14:8

LATE CAREER: 48–60

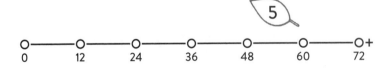

I n 1995, the movie *Braveheart* was released. I was twenty-three and I would have said it was my favorite movie of all time. The hero dies for freedom. "You can take our lives," the William Wallace character cries out, "but you can't take our freedom."[1] When you are twenty-three, you really want to be free. It's the culmination of Day 2.

In 2000, I was twenty-eight, and *Gladiator* hit theaters. I can still remember the visceral effect that movie had on me. I would have said it was my favorite movie of all time. The hero dies to right a great wrong and to depose a false power. Maximus rallies his army with the line, "What we do in life echoes in eternity."[2] When you are close to thirty, you want your life to count; you want to change the world. It is the culmination of Day 3 and the hope of Day 4.

As I write this, I have just turned forty-eight and am now stepping into my own Day 5. What is my all-time favorite movie now? *Jojo Rabbit*. The writer/director Taika Waititi called the movie a love letter to single moms. And without giving too much away (because if you haven't, you should go watch it), the hero dies for doing a small act of resistance in the face of great evil. Facing greater odds than William Wallace's Scotland or Gladiator's Rome, Rosie Betzler models a heroism to her ten-year-old son Jojo, and her soaring exhortation to "do what you can" is the line that echoes in my Day 5 soul. That theme, repeated throughout the movie, is reminiscent of Jesus' own words about the woman from Bethany who anoints His head with perfume: "She did what she could" (Mark 14:8a). And for that small act He would say, "Truly I tell you, wherever the gospel is preached throughout the world, what she has done will also be told, in memory of her" (Mark 14:9). When you are forty-eight, you want your life to get a little smaller, while figuring out the small things that matter most.

It might just be me, but the epic, even muscular, nature of the first two movies is also lost on me now. *Jojo Rabbit* is playful, strange, and almost impossible to categorize. It defies genre in the same way that life (to the Day 5 mind) defies simple categories. The movie is as deep as any, but also funny and tender and chilling. It is not melodrama. It is visually light, yet set on the backdrop of one of the darkest times in human history. In fact, Waititi makes a conscious choice to paint a World War II movie (almost always dark) in bright colors. This kind of juxtaposition reveals, at least for me, the yearning of Day 5. To find joy and love and light in the midst of the battle that is life. You do not exit Day 4 without some scars. Usually a limp. But you also do not exit Day 4 without some substance either. It is in the acceptance of both of these realities that we gain not just perspective, but depth.

GRAVITAS

Craig Barnes, in *The Pastor as Minor Poet*, refers to this quality of depth as gravitas:

> The old seminary professors used to speak about a necessary trait for pastoral ministry called gravitas. It refers to a soul that has developed enough spiritual mass to be attractive, like gravity. It makes the soul appear old, but gravitas has nothing to do with age. It has everything to do with wounds that have healed well, failures that have been redeemed, sins that have been forgiven, and thorns that have settled into the flesh. These severe experiences with life expand the soul until it appears larger than the body that contains it. Then it is large enough to proclaim a holy joy, which is what makes the pastor's soul so attractive.[3]

It is in Day 5, if we have kept our hand to the plow, that our soul will begin to appear larger than the body that contains it. It comes to us through experience, and experience comes to us through both success and failure. We do not gain gravitas without failure. Yet, there is a vast difference between unreckoned failure and repentance. For all of us sinners, the goal is not perfection but reckoning. Can you face, own, and internalize your failures? The one who does gains gravitas. It is as plain as the nose on their face.

> **For all of us sinners, the goal is not perfection but reckoning.**

In Jesus, the gospel writers called it authority. All who came in contact with Him could not help but notice His ease with children, His nerve before power, His gentle fearlessness, and the way He spoke about God. They knew they were witnessing something rare. "When the crowd saw this, they were filled with awe; and they praised God, who had given such authority to man" (Matt. 9:8). His soul always appeared larger than the body that contained it. He was always moving people by His invisible, celestial gravity, pulling some in and throwing some out. Day 5 may be the closest we get to that same quality. Spiritual authority, like any gift, has to be stewarded. And stewardship is always mitigated by our will to give.

CORE DEVELOPMENTAL CONCEPT FOR DAY 5

GIVING

Erik Erikson has given us the term "generativity"[4] to describe the stage of adulthood where we begin to seriously think about the next generation. This desire to see the next generation established and thriving is itself a signifier of an important developmental change. A simpler, more biblical term might be generosity. The urge to give, particularly to those who are coming behind us, should grow and bloom in Day 5, and with it, the emerging desire to leave something behind. Giving marks this stage of our growth and development.

Teaching is giving. Writing is giving. Empowering leadership is giving. Not just sharing, but giving away knowledge you have gained, power you have accumulated, and access you have earned is at the heart of generativity. This Day, then, should be a time of what Erikson called "procreativity" as a space between the creative work of Day 4 and the legacy work of Day 6. Concerned with both "productivity, and creativity, and thus the generation of new beings as well as of new products and new ideas,"[5] we become concerned with the scaling of our creative work while also wanting to see the next generation flourish.

The work of creation (Day 4) is bringing something into the world that was not there before. The work of giving is seeing that creative gift given away as widely as possible. The developmental focus of someone in Day 5 changes from being concerned about the birth of an idea or community to the scattering of that contribution to as many people as possible. This happens best when it is carried on by others. Flowers cover great fields because their pollen is carried on by the bees that have tasted the gift of their nectar. Nurture and propagation go hand in hand. The generous heart, cultivated on this Day, will multiply grace exponentially.

EMPOWERMENT AS GIVING

In his unique and semiautobiographical book, *Orbiting the Giant Hairball*, Gordon MacKenzie, one of the most creative and enigmatic executives corporate America has ever produced, tells the story of his last three years at Hallmark. MacKenzie—his gravitas, derived from having shaped the creative culture of the organization for so long and being a brave and playful innovator—was given total freedom to design a job for himself. True to form, he gave himself the title "Creative Paradox," leaving everyone in the organization to wonder about not only what his job actually was but also where he fit in the org chart.

By design, MacKenzie reveled in the ambiguity. People were never sure how important he was and so assigned him C-suite status, even though he held no actual line management or decision-making power. What he chose to do with his time and mysterious power was as remarkable as he was. Over time, Hallmark employees learned that if you had an idea, you should bring it to the Creative Paradox. He would help you. And if he signed off on it, there was real traction for it. Line managers all over the company found themselves thinking, "If the Creative Paradox supports her idea, maybe I'd better support it too."[6] He describes his daily work this way:

> *Tap tap tap.* A visitor would peer tentatively through the open door in my darkened room. . . .
>
> I would become 136 years old.
>
> "*Come,*" I would beckon frailly to my visitor.

"*Sit,*" I would whisper, gesturing toward the three directors' chairs just inside the door.

We would sit in silence a moment, allowing an air of sacredness to emerge. Then, finally:

"*Tell me,*" I would open.

The visitor would describe the idea.

"*Good idea,*" I would pronounce. . . .

"*Thank you,*" the visitor would smile. And leave. Ratified.

I did that for *three* years. The last three of my 30 at Hallmark I had no job description and a job title that had no meaning. And yet they were the most enriching, fruitful, productive, joy-filled years of my entire career.

Talk about paradox.[7]

This is a wonderful picture of generativity and the empowerment impulse behind it. Thirty years of gravitas, influence, and experience consolidated into the simple gesture of saying yes to people. What Gordon MacKenzie had to give, he set up his life to give away. An excellent example of gravitas coupled with generativity and the virtue of giving, qualities which are so important for Day 5 development.

IDEAL DEVELOPMENTAL CONDITION FOR DAY 5

SCALE

The wise painter, who has pioneered a new style of painting, will not spend their Day 5 selling their paintings; they will spend it teaching that style to a new generation of young painters. In turn, the world will not just have a few more paintings with that strange new style; it will be filled with painters filling the world with paintings inspired by it. This is the economy of scale and is at the heart of the impact that will most move us in Day 5.

> The ideal conditions for a flourishing mentor provides space to take the unique thing they have created and multiply it.

Days 4, 5, and 6 consist of a narrowing, or specializing, each Day becoming more focused than the one before it. The ideal conditions for a flourishing mentor provides space to take the unique thing they have created and multiply it, somehow growing it, expanding it, and giving it more fully to the world. That will mean refusing to do anything (professionally) that does not accomplish this end. In order to bring something to scale, you have to simplify it. So too with the creative work of your life. Day 5 will require even further specialization.

MY STORY

The creative work of my Day 4 was the UNDERGROUND Network. So now, that complex matrix of ideas, systems, people, and the mysterious work of God now exists where it once did not. As I move into Day 5, my eyes are drawn to the horizon of the world beyond my world. In many ways, the work of creation (Day 4) requires intense local focus. To write a book, raise a child, start a group, build a house, or paint a painting means moving from the big picture to the small. You have to bear down and do it. Thinking too much about the world beyond that creative project will diminish the finished product.

But once it is made and our contribution has been offered, we can and should look up from our work and see the world beyond. This outward gaze asks the question: Are there other people and places that need what I have made? For me, that means thinking about how I can give away our story, the hope it brings, and the hard fought lessons of building a new form of the church. That does not have to be systematic, and for me it almost certainly will not be. But part of my Day 5 call will be to give the creative gift away to leaders around the world—a journey that has already begun in earnest. But scaling the idea does not mean scaling the work itself. For instance, in our case, the story can be given away freely without the more cumbersome work of building some kind of global brand. That would certainly count as scaling but so too something more simple and relational.

PRIMARY DEVELOPMENTAL THREAT FOR DAY 5

DISTRACTION

For Erikson, the opposite of generativity is stagnation. This continuum between generativity and stagnation is related to our contribution beyond the scope of our lives. It is not a question of activity. In other words, it is very possible to be busy and even productive but not in a way that is generous. It is possible to be doing a lot while also stagnating. In this sense, stagnation has only to do with the investment we are making in the next generation and in the life of our ideas beyond the scope of our own work.

Therefore, the primary developmental threat for Day 5 is not that we would stop working but that we would not work on the right things. I call this threat distraction because while Day 5 demands we think beyond the opportunities and disappointments that are right in front of us, they are also notoriously hard to ignore. These distractions take both forms and must be contended with in their own right. Focusing on these two dynamic realities (opportunity and disappointment) instead of giving away what we have is equivalent to Day 5 stagnation.

OPPORTUNITY COST

When you are young, your world is small, and you yearn for it to grow bigger. It is at this point, between Day 4 and 5, that your world has grown big, and you want it to grow smaller. Ironically, this is also likely to be at the height of your impact. It is possible that you will have more meaningful opportunities than you have time. Day 5, then, is fraught with the peril of too many open doors. And yet the primary threat to someone in Day 5 is that they still think of themselves in Day 4. That is not to say we are not still creating and seizing opportunity. Of course, those paths remain open to us, but the greater satisfaction will be found in giving yourself away and in giving yourself away to the right people and the right opportunities.

The best parents are present in the lives of their kids. They are involved but not overbearing. Too many of us know what it is like to grow up with parents who were just not there. Oftentimes, that absence directly correlates to business or career success. We sacrificed one thing for the other. When our kids most need us, we are often most absent. Day 5 is a bit like that. We will find ourselves facing the same kind of dilemma. At the zenith of our influence, we will also find ourselves surrounded by younger people who are themselves capable of leadership and looking to make their mark on the world. A shift in our own self-understanding can mean a windfall for those young leaders. A refusal to make such a shift can also mean that we are absent as mentors for them. However sad that is for them, it is worse for us, because it is those young leaders who should become some of the most important people for us in Day 5.

Hypothetically, let's say my story is one of coming out of addiction. In my late 20s, I find a great addiction ministry to work with as a way of serving a greater call I feel to help people who are trapped in the same way I was. In my early 30s, I begin to see shortfalls in the way we work with people. I have some new ideas fueled by my frustration with a system. So, I begin Day 4 by starting a new ministry. Or writing a new process curriculum, something I consider to be a new way of working through addiction. Throughout my late 30s and early 40s, I work to share those ideas and am overjoyed to see the impact they are having, not just on people with addictions but on the people who are called to work with them.

At the end of my 40s, as I enter Day 5, I might find myself more in demand than ever before. What used to feel like an uphill climb, convincing people about my ideas, now seems easy. I have more and more opportunities to teach, partner with other organizations, and even build my own brand. Yet, at the same time, I have a group of leaders and potential leaders connected with me. Whether I see it or not, I am facing an important dilemma. I can chase as many of those opportunities as possible (continuing to think like someone in Day 4), or I can invest more in the leaders around me. If I do the former, in the short term I will see my personal influence grow and my ideas spread. But in the long term, I am actually dooming them to die.

> **The more our creative contribution is tied to us as individuals the more vulnerable that contribution is to decline.**

If I chase the opportunities and neglect mentoring, I will soon find myself alone, and my ideas will die with me. On the other hand, if I pass on what I have and invest in other leaders at the height of their creative contribution, I stand to leave a greater legacy. The more our creative contribution is tied to us as individuals the more vulnerable that contribution is to decline. If I resist some of those distractions, concentrate on giving away what I have learned, and understand myself as moving into a season of mentorship, the result is that my contribution will live on and in this example, more people will be loved through and out of their addictions. The motive here is not solely for the people we are investing in (a sensibility that will mature in Day 6), it is also for the expansion and scaling of my contribution.

If Day 4 is about obtaining achievement, then Day 5 is about stewarding it. Your hard-earned experience and your unique contribution are what now open doors, but the greater satisfaction is found in using that influence to open doors for others.

I realize that this may well rub against professional advice and even personal instincts you are likely to feel at this stage of life. I am not claiming this is the best thing to do for your career or your earning potential. It may be that to take this path will mean leaving some very enticing opportunities on the table. It may mean earning less or passing on invitations that would have seemed like moonshots only a few years ago. All I am claiming is that this is the better path developmentally. If you want to grow, and ultimately to look at the whole of your life with satisfaction and joy, this is the better way. Remembering the words Jesus Himself said: "It is more blessed to give than to receive" (Acts 20:35).

LOOMING DISAPPOINTMENTS

The other form that the threat of distraction may take in Day 5 is disappointment, because in many ways the dreams of Day 4 are left unsatisfied. I don't want to spoil it for you, especially if you are in or entering Day 4. Maybe it is best to just put the book down and plan to pick it back up in a decade. But for those who have tried to create something, to see light break out in some dark place, there is a fraternity of failure, disappointment, and grace that you will soon join. Because of sin, the world now resists creation. And when we take part in that renewing work of Day 4, we find out just how resistant the world can be. Art and beauty do come, but they come through a maze of twists and turns, surprise and heartbreak. Still, once the dust settles from that extraordinarily important day, we will no doubt have both triumph and tragedy to reflect on. Avoid the temptation to choose just one. They are both important and both a kind of revelation about the ongoing mission of God, which fights through our sin and setbacks. Redemption never comes cheap. If pain is what you are feeling in this transition, have the courage to open your eyes and see the glory of the last day. It is there. And if you are more prone to denying the wounds you now carry, have the courage to run your fingers over those scars and to thank God for them.

There is a wonderful moment, so easily overlooked in the life of Jesus, just after He has risen and before He meets with the disciples in Galilee. The angel announcing His rising tells the women, He "is going ahead of you into Galilee. There you will see him" (Mark 16:7). Jesus could easily have made that journey from the tomb to the meeting place with them, but He seems to want to take this walk alone. I wonder what that walk would have been like, what His prayers would have been, what emotions He might have experienced—from the anguish of the disappointment in Gethsemane and the corresponding anguish of the trials and execution to the triumph and relief of this moment. As promised, He is alive.

Here He stands in that twilight moment you may experience after doing something you set out to do, something so hard you wondered if you could even do it. The latent promise God made that He would see you through it is fulfilled. And now here you are, alone with Him, your thoughts, and the afterglow of having done it. I have taken walks like that, my body full of fatigue, relief, disbelief, and joy. For me this is how we make it through the disappointments that accompany us into Day 5. It is very possible that the dreams that have died can distract us from seeing the miracle of making it through; and more to the point, the ways that the dream was actually realized. Sorrow and celebration can lead us to a new revelation of the commitment God has shown and continues to show toward us. Instead of being distracted by those disappointments, we can hear the words of Psalm 31 with new ears and new conviction, "The LORD be exalted, who delights in the well-being of his servant" (Ps. 35:27).

CALLING AND IDENTITY IN DAY 5

MENTOR

These qualities: authority, experience, influence, and generosity all describe an ideal mentor. Normally when we think about mentorship, we consider it from the demand side. Most of us will have had a deficit of good mentors, and the ones we have had are certain treasures.

One of the perils of a culture that glorifies perpetual youth is that we resist gifts of growing older. To give away the spoils of Day 4 should be an occasion for celebration. To take the role of mentor is a psychosocial, even a spiritual, promotion. But because of our fetish for youth, we can resist this new identity. We might be tempted to hold on too long to what we worked so hard to gain in Day 4. Our money, position, title, influence, networks, even the intellectual property of experiential learning, can become stagnant in Day 5 if we refuse to give them away. We hang on too long to our rainmaker identities because we have wrongly believed that those years of creative productivity are simply better.

We live in a world that is growing increasingly critical. Surely, it was always this way, but the platforms for sharing those criticisms have never been so vast. Not only do we have to stave off the usual volume of critics from within our own circle of relationships (natural and expected), but now we have to manage the hundreds (if not thousands) of potential critics whom we have never met. We so desperately need people with real authority to speak into our lives, to challenge us when we are drifting from the heart of God, but also to steel us against false accusation and spurious criticism. We need spiritual mothers and fathers.

In his stern but vulnerable letter to the Corinthian church, Paul offers a series of challenges responding to immature decisions he has heard they have been making. Yet in it, the heart of a true mentor is unveiled. In this particularly vivid line he defines his own role and responsibility to them, "I am writing this not to shame you but to warn you as my dear children. Even if you had ten thousand guardians in Christ, you do not have many fathers, for in Christ Jesus I became your father through the gospel. Therefore I urge you to imitate me" (1 Cor. 4:14–16).

Criticism born from maturity and love is like medicine for the soul; it does not seek to shame but to free. However, loveless criticism is cancerous to our growth and development. What we need we must also commit to be for others. We still have 10,000 guardians who might have an opinion on our behavior, but we do not have enough spiritual parents. This is the role of the mentor, and it is best embodied on Day 5. If we have been blessed to have men and women in our lives who have filled this role, then we will know just how important it is. If, on the other hand, we have looked in vain for such a person, only now to find ourselves on the precipice of fifty, it is time to lay that down and be for others what we did not have ourselves. In Day 5, we find that who we are called to be is in short supply and just what a world of spiritual orphans most needs.

THE DESCENT OF LEADERSHIP[1]

MY STORY

For nearly thirty years now—the span of Days 2–5—I have been in one spiritual leadership role or another. It has been a journey full of joy, fruit, failure and, sadly, even the bitter gall of betrayal. Betrayal comes in two basic forms: the kind others do to you and the kind you do to yourself. The good news is not that it has all worked out, per se, but that I have at least been paying attention. I have learned. And I tend to agree with the proverb derived from Plutarch: "Education is not the filling of a pail, but the lighting of a fire."[2] Each season of leadership development, maturation, and good old-fashioned experience has set ablaze some new realization about the nature and even the climax of spiritual leadership. Here is what I have discovered.

VISIONARY

At first, I was convinced that leadership was about *bold vision*. The leader, after all, is the one who everyone follows. Christians use words like courageous, visionary, and decisive to define good leaders. So, I wanted to know where the community I was leading should go, and then be the first up the hill we were taking. I could see it, and so I got busy learning how to preach and persuade, define reality, and set the standard.

CHAMPION

The visionary way of leading came to feel inadequate somehow, maybe even a bit hollow. I don't believe it was essentially an exercise in ego at first, but more so as time wore on. Somewhere near the end of my Day 3, it became harder and harder to see the face of Jesus in this style of leadership. It was not one moment, but at some point, I woke up to the idea that leadership was about *empowerment*. Real leaders take the power entrusted to them and share it. They build a bigger table with more seats for more kinds of people with different kinds of voices. The Day 4 focus of leadership changed radically for me to being a champion of others and seeing them shine. Maybe the point is not to lead people to a place, but to a person. Ideas like agency and autonomy became more and more important to me. People should be led by God after all; my work is just to give them permission and to empower them to be what He has called them to be. In that sense, I wanted to invite people into the same kind of leadership agency I was enjoying.

SERVANT

Still, there I was at the top of some imaginary spiritual hierarchy, and that location seemed more and more inappropriate for leadership done in Jesus' name. The paradox of *servant leadership* began to capture my heart and mind. The right place for the spiritual leader is not necessarily in front, or at the top, but behind and beneath. An extension of empowerment, the servant leader could actually drop below the people they lead and understand what Jesus likely meant when He said, "You know that the rulers of the Gentiles lord it over them, and their high officials exercise authority over them. Not so with you" (Matt. 20:25–26). The injunction is total and final; leading through strength and hierarchy is not something that requires moderation, but a radical reversal. The way of Jesus is to serve under and never to "lord over." And so I began to see the development and success of the people I was called to lead as the most important work of leadership. A subjugation of myself, my ideas, and my vision for their growth, health, development, and flourishing.

EMERITUS

It is not that one idea replaces the other, but more so that one refines the other, or perhaps one is built upon the foundation of the other. You have to learn them in order, I think. Each preceding commitment becomes the raw material for the new revelation. As I begin Day 5, I find myself face to face with one final leadership revelation. The highest form of leadership and the most mature expression of the leader: *letting go*. To finally and with a whole heart release the last of your leadership capital to others. The pinnacle of leadership is not to lead at all. The term *emeritus* comes from the Latin and is the past tense of the verb *emereri*, a combination of the prefix *e-*, meaning "out," and *merēre*, meaning "to earn, deserve, or serve."[3] It means to serve out. It has a note of both closure and ongoing connection and is the refinement of servant leadership—to serve your way out of leadership altogether.

> **Letting go too soon is not leadership; it is abdication, even negligence...hanging on too long is not leadership either; it is idolatry.**

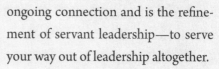

This one might be the hardest and cannot be rushed. Letting go too soon is not leadership; it is abdication, even negligence. But in the same way, hanging on too long is not leadership either; it is idolatry. All the same, this final work of the leader promises one final return on the real currency of leadership, which was never actually power, but joy.

All along, the reason to lead was to know the joy of seeing people come into a life-saving and life-defining relationship with Jesus and to know the joy of intimacy with the one who suffered for us and then let us go. It is to know the joy of experiencing what C. S. Lewis called "the specific pleasure of the inferior."[4] The relationship between kingdom leadership and power, if it is anything, is about letting go of it. We can call this the descent of leadership: taking some power into ourselves, sharing it, and using it for the betterment of others until we finally let it go completely.

And as citizens who have sworn fealty to a crucified God and an upside-down kingdom, this should not surprise us. It turns out that leadership in the kingdom is not an ascent up some ladder, but a descent into Christlikeness.

But figuring out exactly how to embrace this final leadership challenge is neither simple nor obvious. Doing this right means you are just as engaged as at any other phase of leadership. Letting go is not a passive business. It takes serious work. Abandonment is easy. Letting go is an act of generosity and requires the whole heart.

As I have let go of my own leadership over things I started, I have thought about that word from Colossians, that looks like death but feels like home, "For you died, and your life is now hidden with Christ in God" (Col. 3:3). For me, it is not so much about closure, as I am not sure there is such a thing. Ours is an eternal business after all. But it is about fulfillment. Or that wonderful Greek word *teleios*, which in the Bible gets rendered, *complete*, *mature*, and even *perfect*.

This, then, is leadership perfection: to finish something. And to finish is not to end, but to have done your part, to have run your race and to let go of the baton to the next runner in the relay.

DAY 6

THE MYSTIC

"In the evening of your life you will be judged on love."[1]

OSCAR ROMERO

TRANSITION: 60-72+

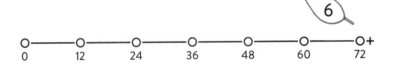

The best we can tell, the longest living disciple was John, and he may have lived into his 90s. This would have been miraculously old for the first century. In fact, his advanced years may have contributed to the widespread rumor at the time that Jesus claimed he would not die. Still, we should all be grateful for John's long life and the late-blooming writing contributions he made. In spite of being exiled to the island of Patmos under the tyrannical reign of Nero, John survived to write a Gospel, his extraordinary Revelation, and likely three epistles.

Even a cursory survey of John's gospel and his epistles reveals one persistent, overarching theme: love. And despite its confounding imagery, the book of Revelation offers us the most mystical and forward-looking piece of Scripture in all the Bible. It could be argued that these two themes, or vantage points, would have been underdeveloped in the New Testament without him. These two areas of fascination—mysticism and love—are endemic to Day 6.

In his final years, John seemed to grow more and more fixated and even obsessed with the love of God . . . perhaps, because he had become more aware of that love finding a home in his own heart. And similarly, he seemed to find new heights of intimacy and understanding about the world to come, revelation that was the direct result of deep and luxurious prayer. In the last days of his life, he found himself fascinated by both mystery and love. All of us, as we enter Day 6, can hope for the same fascination as our calling and development takes one final turn toward a panoramic perspective, primarily lived out in a few important relationships.

The work of the final Day, then, like day six of creation, is about people. On day six, God makes human beings in His image. And so, on Day 6 of our creative lives, we look for a small group of people to impart the full blessing and gift of our leadership legacy. This last Day is about investing in a few truly worthy people who can be the repository of our best learning and our highest care and support. But, like day six of creation, it is also about union, or in our case, re-union. About the impending promise of God walking again with us in the cool of the day and our gaze turning, for the first time, away from this world and on to the next.

CORE DEVELOPMENTAL CONCEPT FOR DAY 6

LEAVING/FINISHING

Given the advances in modern medicine, as of 2017, the world life expectancy age was 72.2, up from 67.2 in 2010 and 47 in 1950.[2] Of course, many of us will live well beyond, and too many will die well before the age of 72, but this number gives us an ending point for our discussion. We all have to face the finality of our lives and at least concede, if not celebrate, that we will finish what we have started. This notion of leaving, or finishing, is crucial to our developmental understanding of the last years of our lives. These years

Leaving is not the same as finishing.

can't be like any others, precisely because they are the last. They constitute the nature and content of our ending. In that sense, it does not matter how we conceive these years; it is how we live them that defines our exit.

Over the course of my career, I have left several positions. In each case, I had the luxury of some time to consider, plan, and set exit goals. Because I treasured both the work I had done as well as the people who would continue that work in my absence, I was always eager to finish as well as I possibly could. In one case, my exit plan took two years. There were simply things I wanted to be able to leave behind for my successors before I could feel good about my exit. Leaving is not the same as finishing. Books needed to be balanced, relationships transferred, hires put in place, and looming challenges resolved. You may have had a similar experience. Or perhaps you have been on the other side of an abrupt or ill-conceived exit. The alternative is to leave your successors with a wheel to reinvent or a mess to clean up.

In his book *Tuesdays with Morrie*, Mitch Albom lovingly chronicles a series of conversations with his one-time professor and mentor Morrie Schwartz, who was facing a slow decline from Lou Gehrig's disease. The idea that most deeply resonated with me was Morrie's assertion that it was a gift to die slowly. A slow death gives one time to end well. In that sense, all of us who have made it to an advanced age have been given this gift: time to think through not only the way we want to leave our positions and to finish our work, but also how we want to leave this life.

LEADERS WHO DON'T FINISH WELL

As I write this, alarming new claims are being made about yet another well-known Christian leader that will tarnish his legacy. Revelations like these are troubling for two reasons. First, we have vastly overestimated our leaders. We have, perhaps unconsciously, expected that our leaders would lead blameless lives. We are expecting forty to fifty years of ministry without any impropriety. This is not only unlikely, it is unfair. Almost certainly, over so long a period of time, leaders will fail and fall. Sin is ever present in them (as it is with all of us), and it is not a matter of if they will, but when. For me, the more important question is how they respond when they do. Still, we know that our leaders are human beings, and that all human beings are going through their own unique battle with sin and evil. We should not therefore be shocked when those truths are brought into focus by particular improprieties. I am not saying we should not address these errors, or that they aren't at times disqualifying, only that we should not be surprised. And depending on the severity, we should be ready to offer mercy, correction, healing, and restoration in increasing measure.

Second, we find these stories surprising because we do not realize just how hard it is to finish well.

Exploring the theme of lifelong leadership, Robert Clinton has argued that two out of three Christian leaders do not finish well.[3] The catalog of reasons includes losing a learning posture, not paying attention to their character, no longer living by their once stated convictions, failing to leave ultimate contributions, no longer walking in the awareness of their influence, and losing their once flourishing relationship with God. It occurs to me that all of these dynamics have to do with perseverance.

Perseverance often fails because we miss so many of the key transitions I have already outlined. When our lives are not renewed by the fresh calling of a new day, we feel unnecessary fatigue. When we find ourselves worn down, frustrated, or bored by the expectations of Day 4 and 5, seeing the work of Day 6 as essentially the same (a continuation), our perseverance is tested. But when a person recognizes that they have crossed yet another threshold into a new calling—a new way of life with new hopes, dreams, and expectations—perseverance is the last thing they need. Often a moral breakdown is an indicator that the leader was not able to discern the last identity crisis, pressing in again to the face of Jesus and finding new meaning in the particulars of the changing assignments of their life. Alternatively, when we can see this last transition clearly, we can find a moral and spiritual second wind, committing anew to God and His plan for us. We will finish well if we understand the demands and joys of being in the last Day of our life.

Old age does not preclude newness. On the contrary, whatever the quality of the life you have lived, if you have made it this far, you will have attained something precious: perspective. The last Day can, and should, be full of wide-eyed amazement as well as steely conviction. By reflecting on the frailty of our own work and the mistakes we have made, as well as the grace of God coursing through it all, we can find ourselves exhibiting the qualities of a sage and a mystic. This is just as it should be.

IDEAL DEVELOPMENTAL CONDITION FOR DAY 6

CELEBRATION

I am choosing the word celebration here as a proxy for two combined experiences: wisdom and happiness. To celebrate something requires taking an accounting of that thing and then declaring it good. It is to be happy in reflection. This is the ideal condition for our emotional, spiritual, and psychological development on Day 6. To be able to access what we have seen and done, and to somehow find happiness and love in its summation.

In his final months, British neurologist, historian, and author Oliver Sacks was asked to reflect on his life and nearing death in a series of *New York Times* essays, posthumously published in the book called *Gratitude*. In it he writes,

My father, who lived to 94, often said that the 80s had been one of the most enjoyable decades of his life. He felt, as I begin to feel, not a shrinking but an enlargement of mental life and perspective. One has had a long experience of life, not only one's own life, but others', too. One has seen triumphs and tragedies, booms and busts, revolutions and wars, great achievements and deep ambiguities, too. One has seen grand theories rise, only to be toppled by stubborn facts. One is more conscious of transience and, perhaps, of beauty. At 80, one can take a long view and have a vivid, lived sense of history not possible at an earlier age. I can imagine, feel in my bones, what a century is like, which I could not do when I was 40 or 60. I do not think of old age as an ever grimmer time that one must somehow endure and make the best of, but as a time of leisure and freedom, freed from the factitious urgencies of earlier days, free to explore whatever I wish, and to bind the thoughts and feelings of a lifetime together.[4]

Similar to the final conditions outlined by James Fowler in his *Stages of Faith*, we see this coupling of wisdom and happiness in the "mystical-communal,"[5] or what he calls the final stage of maturing faith. For Fowler, mystery follows the acknowledgment of paradox (perhaps a Day 5 discovery). I think this is what the Bible would call wisdom. We see, through experience, that great truths are not binary but come to us as companions, or paradoxes. The Nobel Prize–winning physicist Niels Bohr put it this way, "There are trivial truths and there are great truths. The opposite of a trivial truth is plainly false. The opposite of a great truth is also true."[6] This discovery softens us and makes us more open to the people we might once have regarded as enemies. This can lead to the final stage of faith Fowler calls universalizing. We start to see the people around us as both flawed and worthy. And what is fascinating to me is that for Erikson, who was himself not a man of faith, this final stage is best captured and explained by the experience of love.

For Erikson, the whole arc of our lives can be seen through the virtues of hope, faith, and love. Of course, it was the apostle Paul who first contended that "these three remain" (1 Cor. 13:13a). But, Erikson observed this temporal dynamic: that youth is characterized by hope, midlife is characterized by faith, and a well-ended life is driven and defined by love.

Paul would agree, at least, that "the greatest of these is love" (1 Cor. 13:13b). And it is a comforting and motivating thought to imagine that we are growing up into love. Love is a good rubric for Day 6 exactly because of its complexity. Love implies deep knowledge and even acceptance of imperfection. This comes from experience and wisdom. But it also implies a contentment with the object of our love; that is to say, to love something is to be pleased with it. To love is to hold something or someone in your heart as prized, desired, and precious. In that sense, love is both suffering and happiness. But the final condition is happiness.

HAPPINESS

This happiness is somewhat counterintuitive. The people who have lived the longest should, in one estimation, be the most depressed. They have seen and experienced the most sadness, loss, failure, and betrayal. But just the opposite turns out to be true. Researchers like Andrew Oswald have found that happiness in our lives tends to follow a U shape.[7]

The pattern of a typical person's happiness through life[8]

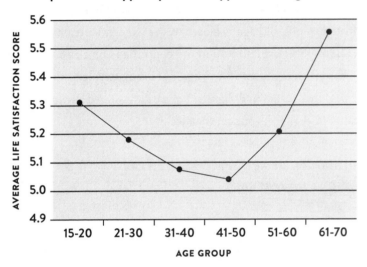

We are happiest in the beginning and end of our lives. In his far reaching research, which included half a million people across seventy-two countries (both developed and developing), Oswald observed the same pattern. Happiness starts to decline in our teen years, finds its low point in our mid-40s, and then steadily rises as we age. Contradicting the notion that older people are less happy than younger, the research reveals that people are their happiest in their 60s and 70s. Against all odds, Day 6 proposes to be our happiest season of life. Bringing to mind the insightful, if cynical, observation in Shakespeare's "As You Like It,"

"Last scene of all,
That ends this strange eventful history,
Is second childishness . . ."[9]

It is true enough that we can, if healthy, return to the happiness we last knew as children. I appreciate this insight because of its symmetry. It is from God we come and to Him we will return. In that sense, old age is closer to the existential reality of early childhood. It brings to mind the contrarian's revelation of G. K. Chesterton in my favorite chapter of his masterpiece, *Orthodoxy*, called the "Ethics of Elfland": "For we have sinned and grown old, and our Father is younger than we."[10]

PRIMARY DEVELOPMENTAL THREAT FOR DAY 6

OBSCURITY

Even though, on average, we are happier when we are older, there are plenty of people who find increased sadness and even depression in their later years. When this happens, the cause is often because of two great losses: the loss of significance and the loss of meaningful relationships. As the funnel of important relationships narrows, the opportunity for mentoring and spiritual parenting increases, but so does the threat of loneliness.

Where once we were central to the lives of a great number of people (our kids, employees, even friends), we can find ourselves on the periphery. This is not in itself a problem. That movement is both natural and healthy. Our kids, for instance, will move out and move on, forming their own families, raising their own kids, and slaying their own dragons. This is as it should be. But it does not diminish the loss of professional (if not personal) significance we will almost certainly feel. The company we once ran, the organization we once chaired, the group we once led have all moved on, and this too is how it should be. A smaller circle can feel like a great loss, especially when our time is simply not as full as it once was. The extra time can lead to either a luxurious introspection culminating in gratitude or an excruciating rumination resulting in bitterness and insignificance.

The journey toward obscurity, while a threat to the ego, is actually good for the soul. A growing insignificance in one arena can unveil greater significance in another. Jesus Himself took such a journey and found exaltation, and a deeper identity at the end. Still, the feeling of being sidelined, overlooked, and ignored at a time in your life when you may well feel you have the most to give, can feel jarring. When you are most full of self-understanding and wisdom it can seem that no one is asking for your input anymore.

> The journey toward obscurity, while a threat to the ego, is actually good for the soul.

Overcoming the "feeling" of obscurity is one thing, but dealing with the reality of loneliness is another. Being sidelined and obscured is only a problem if you are still coveting that central role. That kind of backward gaze is a danger to growth, happiness, and development on Day 6. Obscurity as a psychological implication is only superseded by the physical one. Loneliness is dangerous, in more ways than one. It is associated with early mortality and has been implicated in just about every medical problem you can imagine, including cardiovascular incidents, personality disorders, psychosis, and cognitive decline. Loneliness increases the production of stress hormones and can double the likeliness of developing Alzheimer's disease. One study quantified it this way: loneliness is worse for your health than smoking fifteen cigarettes per day.[11]

NEVER ALONE

One of my oldest and best friends is a raging extrovert. Wildly successful in all he does, he loves people and people love him. He has that unique ability to greet fifty people at a party and leave them all feeling that they are special to him. In an unexpected twist, he also possesses the deepest prayer life of anyone I know. He regularly and effortlessly spends hours in the presence of God.

> God is a friend who waits for us in the place of prayer.

Some years ago, we decided to write a book together. We borrowed a house on a lake and spent a week together, talking and writing. I wake up pretty early, but he was always up before me. I watched him pray for two hours every morning, always wondering how someone so seemingly addicted to *not* being alone could press into such a lonely discipline.

Finally, I asked him, "Mike, you are the biggest extrovert I know. How is it that you can also spend so much time alone in prayer? It makes no sense."

Tilting his head, he gave me that look you get when someone thinks you have lost the plot. "Because I am not alone."

Here is the truth we must finally learn if we are to grow into the fullest possible maturity on Day 6: God is a friend who waits for us in the place of prayer. In that one, sustaining relationship, we are never alone.

Very late in life, John was exiled to the island of Patmos. It was in this place of isolation and solitude that he encountered Jesus in a new way. It was in obscurity that John saw what human beings have struggled to see for 2,000 years since—what the coming of the King would look like. It is because he is alone that he encounters Jesus in this way. The isolation sets the stage for the revelation. And, of course, he is not alone at all. He keeps company with the resplendent presence of a risen and glorified Jesus. This is the deep revelation of mystery, union, and love that comes to us perhaps most clearly when life has slowed down. That revelation, in part, is that our loneliness is a lie and that when we draw close to our best friend and truest companion, there are wonders waiting. It makes me think of that silver line in Mark 4, "But when he was alone with his own disciples, he explained everything" (Mark 4:34b). It may just be that to find ourselves finally alone with Him is to also finally to understand Him, ourselves, and the circumstances of our lives in a new way.

CALLING AND IDENTITY IN DAY 6

MYSTIC

In his book *Sacred Fire*, Ronald Rolheiser explores these same Day 6 transitions through the lens of discipleship. He argues that we go through three grand movements as disciples of

Jesus. Essential discipleship (getting our lives together), mature discipleship (giving our lives away), and radical discipleship (giving our deaths away). The final gesture of discipleship is to "integrate generativity with dying."[12]

If the focus of Day 5 is generativity, or a concern for giving something to the next generation, then Day 6 is concerned with eternity: that is, not just what we leave behind, but what we are stepping into. Of course, for the believer, death is not the end of our lives. If Jesus and the prophets are to be believed, to die in this world is to be welcomed into one that is far greater, with a scope and significance that will make this life seem small. (See James 4:14.)

The next transition facing those of us in Day 6 is the vastest by far. Contemplating our past, as sprawling as that may seem, is still nothing compared to the apprehension of eternity. So it is that we begin to consider not just the lessons of life already lived but the wonder of eternal life that lies before us. In this time when we turn to Jesus for identity and direction, we find new gifts from new questions. How does one prepare for life after death? How does one prepare for union with God? How does one consider calling in the light of fruition? All those questions take on new meaning and offer us new insight into the answer to not just one of them, but all of them at the same time. The way to prepare for eternity is to draw near to the One who governs it. The way to prepare for this next transition is to hold the hand of the only One we know who is already there.

Intimacy with God can and should take on new meaning for us as we walk through the months and years of Day 6. Each day that draws us closer to our end is a day closer to finally seeing Him. There is certainly grief in the loss of what we will leave behind, but that is true in every transition.

Every transition between Days is a kind of death and an end of something. It is only the coming newness of the subsequent Day that can soften this sense of loss. Still, often this transition feels like a grief. Because in many ways we grieve the end of one thing as we welcome the beginning of another. But this is the fullness of the purpose and promise of the life, death, and rising of Jesus. Death is never the end for us. Because of Jesus, death always becomes life. You just have to wait a while. And take those next steps—the way of Jesus extending before you.

For most of us reading these words (and me as I write), this season of life is not something we have experienced personally. We might be tempted to think about this final Day as something dreadful, if only for its proximity to dying. But this is not what those who are dying actually report. Recent research reveals that instead of feeling fear and regret, people close to death experience something entirely more positive. Two studies in particular, one looking at the blog posts of near-death patients and the other at death row inmates, uncover some remarkable commonalities in late life experience.[13]

Researcher and social scientist Kurt Gray explains:

> When we imagine our emotions as we approach death, we think mostly of sadness and terror.... But it turns out, dying is less sad and terrifying.
>
> In our imagination, dying is lonely and meaningless, but the final blog posts of terminally ill patients and

the last words of death row inmates are filled with love, social connection, and meaning.[14]

Applying a technique called content analysis, Gray and his colleagues were able to both quantify and qualify the emotional intent of the writers. They also compiled writing samples from a control group of non-patients writing through a simulated emotional experience by imagining imminent death.

It is not just that they uncovered that those who are closer to the end of their lives were more positive, reflective, grateful, and sentimental; but that the way the rest of us think about that time is wrong. Even this is hard for those of us who are not yet there to understand. But it seems that when we look back, we feel more gratitude and love than we do regret and fear.

And so it is that the threshold upon which we now stand is full of mystery. If looking back can fill us with love, then looking forward will fill us with wonder. This dual perspective of retrospection and awe has the potential to turn us all into mystics because having one foot in this world and one in the world to come will create a kind of panoramic point of view. Even the most pragmatic people, when standing in between these two realities, will become fountains of insight and presence. The mentor becomes the mystic.

The aging and death I have witnessed most closely was my maternal grandfather. A distinguished, even elegant man; his heart remained a secret to most of us. A decorated World War II pilot, successful executive, and devoted husband and father, he was deeply private. Despite being a faithful church attender, he was otherwise quiet about the things of God. I can vividly remember that when my fire for God was just beginning to burn, he began to open up to me about his. When I sensed a call to ministry, he shared his own call he had felt as a young man. He was then, and is still, a mystery to me. But we became closer and closer as age and death crept up on him, and I never felt more intimacy with him than when he was very near the end.

I think he knew that this final stage of life was a doorway to knowing God in a new way, and the intensity of this stage matched the intensity of mine. But his advice, insight, and even our ordinary conversations took on significance beyond their meaning. I could sense he was closer than I was to my own heart's desire—Jesus. He was always a mentor to me, but in those last months, he became a mystic.

The ending of his life reminds me of the end of the sixteenth-century Spanish mystic Teresa of Ávila. A woman renowned for her "raptures," her life was replete with encounters and deep intimacy with God. Yet, she knew that in one sense the Jesus whom she had wed as a Carmelite nun was also someone she had never met face to face—a promise to be fulfilled in death. This paradox is contained in her last words, recorded with her dying breath, "O my Lord and my Spouse, the hour that I have longed for has come. It is time to meet one another."[15] My grandfather's own rejuvenated faith was something he was more eager than ever to share. And I was fortunate enough to be there to receive it.

Building on the revelation of Day 5, we are still concerned about passing on what we know to the next generation. But instead of passing on what we have made, or even what we have learned, there is something deeper being transferred. The mystical mentor offers us themselves. *Tuesdays with Morrie* is a wonderful case study for this kind of relationship. You can see that what is being transferred from Morrie to Mitch is not just ideas or principles but something more transcendent: himself.

Then God said, "Let us make humankind in our image, according to our likeness" (Gen. 1:26 NRSV). Day 6 of creation was a master stroke of perpetuity. God makes a creature with enough of His likeness to be able to not just maintain, but to continue, creating long after He has entered into His rest.

The mystic begins to better understand not only what life was all about, but what it is that keeps it going. The mystic is committed to a full scope of time. When we are in our right mind, we can see that this final transition is not an end for us or the people we leave behind. The story of God and His people is so much more grand than that. This epic perspective makes us want to look for a still narrowing group of people, sometimes even our own kids, to pass on all that we know and all that we are as a final act of generosity and love.

So it is that the mystic becomes acquainted in a new way with the centrality of love. Platitudes about love are everywhere. It is easy to be skeptical about them since any assertion about the importance of love seems so utterly unquestioned. We can be forgiven for feeling like these platitudes are tired and lack sophistication. And as much as I like novelty and insights that seem like breakthroughs, the centrality of love persists. It could well be that our almost universal acceptance of this one virtue is its most compelling argument. Is there another subject with which human beings seem to be in such agreement? Still, like all truths, there is knowing and then there is knowing. Our deepest truths become bumper stickers, trivialized because there is actually something more there to take in.

FINISHING WITH LOVE

The Harvard Study of Adult Development, originally called the Harvard Grant Study, is perhaps the most remarkable and certainly longest running longitudinal study of its kind. Started in 1938, researchers set out to follow the life and careers of 268 Harvard sophomores. For more than eighty years, they have followed this class of men that included the likes of President John F. Kennedy and *Washington Post* editor Ben Bradlee. As of 2017, only a handful of the study participants were still alive,[16] but the data collected over eight decades is stunning, if only for its scope.

George Vaillant joined the team in 1966 and took over the study in 1972. He has written several books from this rich and seemingly endless source material. But even Vaillant, as an observer and commentator, has been changed through the passage of so much time. One of the more remarkable things about a study spanning nearly a century is the way the research itself changes—not only the tools, but also the assumptions and underlying belief systems that have themselves come and gone over the years.

In his book *Triumphs of Experience*, Vaillant builds to a summation of the whole study, including its impact on him. In a sea of data covering more than 1,200 topics, the overarching pursuit of happiness, he concludes, is dependent on two things: "One is love. The other is finding a way of coping with life that does not push love away."[17]

Banish the idea of some inscrutable, levitating guru; the mystic is simply someone who has come to terms with the centrality of love. The great gift of the last Day of life is proximity to this one ultimate truth: "If we love one another, God lives in us and his love is made complete in us" (1 John 4:12).

Of course we are still creating, still mentoring, and for that matter still learning and serving, up until our last breath. Those identities are never lost to us. But the mystic embraces the final Day of life for what it is, an impending reunion with God.

The conviction of the centrality of love is fed by the revelations of a life long lived, and an eternity waiting for us. In the end, this is also the image of God we pass on to our prodigy. We, having been recreated into the image of God, who is love, are then leaving ourselves as an impression on those that are closest to us. We leave a legacy as mystics who drink deeply from the cup of love, perhaps because we know we will soon see His face.

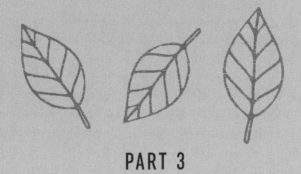

PART 3

7TH DAY REST

TRANSFIGURATION

*"After six days Jesus took Peter, James and John with him
and led them up a high mountain, where they were all alone.
There he was transfigured before them."*

MARK 9:2

For as long as I can remember, speaking in public has been a part of my life. As a child I was a poor student, but as I mentioned at the beginning of the book, my first success in the classroom came while giving a speech about Julius Caesar. I preached my first sermon before a congregation when I was sixteen. More than thirty years of speaking in hundreds of venues before thousands of people, and there is still a stirring in the pit of my stomach just before I stand up. The anxiety of public speaking comes from the dynamics of preparation and delivery. We struggle to find the right words to say, we battle uncertainty and nerves, and then we get up and deliver that questionable content. But there is this other, more mysterious moment in the life of a public speaker, a moment that happens in the hallway before you walk in or in the seat before you stand up. It is the threshold between preparation and execution. It is like that moment right before the time runs out when you're taking a test; you exhale, understanding there is nothing more to be done. I am intimately acquainted with that threshold moment, and, for me, it is a place of peace that only comes through surrender. Surrender to the knowledge that you have done what you could, and now it is in God's hands. I really love that moment . . . standing in the corridor, alone, no longer striving. It is the space between preparation and judgment.

Jesus died so that when we come to that threshold between this life and the next, we can find ourselves strangely at peace with our own death. We do not "rage against the dying of the light"[1] because we know He has gone before us to prepare a place. And so we stand, finally, at the precipice of that new life. Death is that threshold and should only be feared by those who have chosen to rely on their own righteousness to prepare them. "For you died, and your life is now hidden with Christ in God. When Christ, who is your life, appears, then you also will appear with him in glory" (Col. 3:3–4).

All we can reliably know about life after death must come from the One who has mastered them both. Jesus who lived, died, and rose to eternal life is "the firstborn from among the dead" (Col. 1:18). And He who has conquered death has promised a 7th Day that will be more wondrous than we can possibly imagine.

In culmination of our exploration of development, I offer three of these promises concerning that still veiled reality to come: it will be a place of reward, rest, and reign.

REWARD

One of the more remarkable, yet often overlooked characteristics of Jesus' life and ministry was His apparent introversion, perhaps even shyness. For most of His adult life, He simply lay low. Even after He burst onto the scene doing miracles and gathering massive crowds throughout Galilee, He was often trying to evade and escape the throng of the crowd. Even more, He consistently gave instructions to the recipients of one of His miracles (presumably the people most poised to spread the word about Him) to keep it to themselves. Jesus seems eager to keep what scholars call "the messianic secret." His attempt to maintain a low profile, and de facto, God's intent to keep His incarnation shrouded in humanity, gives us a Jesus we can better relate to. Still, the man Jesus was also God, walking in disguise in our world. The fullness of His deity was not something He wanted to use as a lever for belief or allegiance. As Paul would explain, He took "the very nature of a servant" (Phil. 2:7). And those who would believe in Him would have to believe in Him in that form. There is, however, one remarkable exception. An episode that has come to be known simply as the transfiguration stands alone as a moment that reveals Jesus as something entirely other than human. And the reason we know about it is because three of His friends were allowed to witness it.

I find it strangely important that this revelation comes to them just after Jesus predicts His death: one crushing revelation followed by an exalting one. And this revelation comes to them, in the words of Mark, "after six days" (Mark 9:2). Of course, the passing of six days is important, not just to Mark but to us. It is a full week that has passed, and it is at the end of that length of time, the same length of time with which the Father made the world, that Jesus is revealed to them as something other than a suffering servant.

"After six days Jesus took Peter, James and John with him and led them up a high mountain, where they were all alone. There he was transfigured before them" (Mark 9:2).

And so it is that after the Six Days of our lives, Jesus will take us to the place of full and final transfiguration. The secret of His identity will be fully and finally revealed, the role of faith no longer necessary, as the undeniable reality of His glorious person will be ours to behold. Whatever there is to say about life after death, this much is promised. We will behold Him. And we will know fully, even as we are fully known.

For those who love Him, whose whole life (whether we were always aware of it or not) was a yearning to be with Him, this represents the greatest possible reward. Every time we felt sad, alone, broken, torn, ashamed, or afraid, we were really waiting for this moment—to behold someone so utterly beautiful, so totally whole, that our every tear would be wiped away. Once and for all. This, then, is the first connotation of the 7th Day. It is a reward for a life lived under the banner of His love and dependent on His grace. Just as the transfiguration was a kind of reward to Peter, James, and John for staying with Him in spite of an impending crucifixion, so too we will be rewarded for holding fast until the end.

In Revelation, John chooses the image of a wedding to describe the emotional dimension of Jesus as reward. A wedding is a place of transformation, two people becoming one. It is a place of celebration, as that union is an occasion for joy. It is a place of mystery, as unbreakable promises are made. And it is a place of intimacy, as two people who have wanted to know each other fully now finally can. The culmination of the whole saga is union—to look upon Him, our love and our great reward.

REST

We have all felt soul-weary. Tired in a way that we know a good night's rest or a vacation can't help. And in that weariness, there is a corresponding relief that we sense but can't find. And so it is that another connotation for the 7th Day is rest. There is a reason why one billion Buddhists believe this singular premise of their religious worldview, "all life is suffering." There is a reason why Sabbath has been the central governing religious idea for the Jewish diaspora, in constant exile, exhausted by a seemingly never-ending search for home. Life is hard precisely because we are far from God. Life is hard because we make it hard, for ourselves and for each other. Life is hard because sin and death are just as present to us as grace and life. How can the cascading, compounding effects of sin even be put into words? The world we inhabit now is held together by a grace we can't see and certainly do not fully appreciate. But whether it is done to us, or done by us, the disaster and calamity of human sin and suffering will one day, for those who have hidden their lives in Christ, come to an end. The labor of mission, the battle for holiness, the struggle for justice, and the constant pain of irreconciliation will not last forever.

For the Jewish and early Christian mind, this is memorialized in Sabbath rest. Once a week, we remember that someday we will all find that elusive rest for our souls. That weekly ritual stands as a memorial to the day when all our tears will be dried, the nations will be reconciled, and all our pain will be taken away. This connotation is a balm for all who are poor, who are oppressed, and who suffer. It is especially poignant as our bodies grow old and begin to shut down. Rarely do human beings die quietly and without pain. In that sense, the threshold between our two lives highlights the gift of our ultimate Sabbath rest.

"There remains, then, a Sabbath-rest for the people of God; for anyone who enters God's rest also rests from their works, just as God did from his. Let us, therefore, make every effort to enter that rest" (Heb. 4:9–11a).

REIGN

While rest beyond the striving of this life is a reward for the individual, the world remains a place that is untrue to its Creator's intent. Sin has not just marred us, but the whole system. There is a panacea for all human depravity, and it is the rule and reign of Jesus. This then is the final connotation of the 7th Day, that He will reign on the earth, and we will reign with Him.

Jesus has promised that He will return, not just to judge the world, but to restore it. And when He does, He will be accompanied by those who have died in Christ. The rider on the white horse in Revelation 19 is followed by the redeemed, or what Paul calls the "dead in Christ" (Rev. 19:11–21; 1 Thess. 4:16). Life after death then promises to be full of challenge, adventure, and a yet unwritten story. Contrary to popular belief, we will not sit idly on clouds playing harps. This placid and boring notion has left some of us feeling reluctant about a life after death that seems, well, lifeless. The good news is that this idea bears no resemblance to the new life Scripture promises.

On the contrary, we will all play some part in His return and in that long awaited delivery of judgment and justice. He has work to do. The breaking of the seals, the blowing of trumpets, and also the pouring out of bowls all represent passages of time. Whatever we can say about the eschaton, it will not happen all at once. And we will be part of it somehow.

Jesus takes the throne in Revelation 4 as a fulfillment of that ancient promise, sung by the first church, "Therefore God exalted him to the highest place and gave him the name that is above every name, that at the name of Jesus every knee should bow, in heaven and on earth and under the earth, and every tongue acknowledge that Jesus Christ is Lord, to the glory of God the Father" (Phil. 2: 9–11). It is the Lamb, who was slain, who lived as a person, lived with us, ate with us, knew us, taught us, healed us, loved us, and finally died for us . . . this One takes the throne.

Jesus comes into the world the first time to save it. He does not come to condemn it. This is earth-shattering news. It is good news. When God finally appears on the face of His corrupted creation, He does not appear to destroy it or to condemn it, but to speak a tender word of hope and salvation. Further, He knows that it will not be healed without a great display and sacrifice of love. It is love that is His great and unexpected weapon to destroy evil and liberate His children. And so He dies for us. I know you have heard that before and so you are tempted to simply gloss over it. But consider again that He does not come to kill but to die. He does not come to condemn but to save. And to save by throwing Himself upon the gears of the machine.

The conqueror, who first loved the world, will now judge it. He came as a peacemaker. As a sacrificial, servant leader, and now He takes His place as a warrior king. And all that is wrong; all that is defiant; all that hates and lies and lusts and kills; all that denies God and that rejects love's command; all that has set itself up as superior to God; all that has poisoned and betrayed, broken and beaten, envied and taken; all that has stolen and cheated; all that is openly vile, and all that is fashionably bad; all that is unfaithful and untrue . . . must stand and be judged. These things must face the coming of the daystar, the living One. And this is a fierce and dreadful spine-chilling thing. But all this is done in the company of witnesses. We are there. Let that sink in. We are being promoted to a position of witnessing and participating somehow in the summary judgment of evil and the joyful restoration of all things.

For those who are in Christ, not only is death not something to fear, it is something to gain. When reflecting on His own death, perhaps Paul was able to say "to live is Christ and to die is gain" (Phil. 1:21) because of this other word to Timothy, "If we died with him, we will also live with him; if we endure, we will also reign with him" (2 Tim. 2:11–12). We do not just gain an end to our labor and suffering, we do not just find sweet union and peace with God, we also find a timeline stretching out before us, full of leadership, adventure, challenge, and achievement. This is the final promise of the 7th Day.

"Blessed and holy are those who share in the first resurrection. The second death has no power over them, but they will be priests of God and of Christ and will reign with him for a thousand years" (Rev. 20:6).

So it is that the whole of our lives will have been a preparation for this one great task—to reign alongside Him. To have been made worthy by His sacrifice and to see that work finally completed. It is a sumptuous hope that we hold on to, and no matter your age as you read this, no matter your stage of life or development, if you will make Him Lord, this is your wondrous future.

ACKNOWLEDGMENTS

I wrote most of this book while living and working in Ireland, and I owe a debt of love to my friends and colleagues there. Even though the content of this book took many years of observation and research, there was something about that place (and those people) that gave me new insight and the drive to finally make sense of it. Simon and Cheryl Kilpatrick, Michael and Belinda Briggs, as well as the whole Praxis and Ignite communities, thank you for making room in your lives for us and for giving me a place to work out some of these unfinished ideas.

I should also acknowledge my own six children, who have provided my clearest sampling of early childhood and adolescence. Thank you Jael, Noah, Eve, Luke, Simeon, and Skyler for being uniquely you and for teaching us that parenting should fit the child. As always, massive thanks to Alisa Rehn, my tireless assistant who endured every first draft and who carefully vetted all my research. Finally, I am grateful to my Moody editor team Duane Sherman and Amanda Cleary Eastep, who made the whole process easy. Thank you for just the right amount of challenge and affirmation.

NOTES

Introduction: The Fingerprint Paradox

1. William Shakespeare, *As You Like It: A Comedy* (London: S. Gosnell, 1810), 34.

2. Erik H. Erikson, *The Life Cycle Completed*, extended version with new chapters on the ninth stage of development by Joan M. Erikson (New York: W. W. Norton & Company, 1998).

3. Ibid., 55.

4. James W. Fowler, *Stages of Faith: The Psychology of Human Development and the Quest for Meaning* (San Francisco: HarperOne, 1995).

5. Data from James W. Fowler, *Stages of Faith: The Psychology of Human Development and the Quest for Meaning* (San Francisco: HarperOne, 1995).

6. George E. Vaillant, *Triumphs of Experience: The Men of the Harvard Grant Study* (Cambridge, MA: The Belknap Press of Harvard University Press, 2015).

7. Erikson, *The Life Cycle Completed*, 66.

8. David G. Benner, *Surrender to Love—Discovering the Heart of Christian Spirituality* (Downers Grove, IL: IVP, 2015), 95–96.

Part 1: Dynamic Calling

1. "I have come that [you] may have life" (John 10:10).

2. Friedrich Wilhelm Nietzsche, *Beyond Good and Evil: Prelude to a Philosophy of the Future* (Hampshire, UK: Macmillan, 1907), 107.

Day 1: The Child

1. Frederick Buechner, *Wishful Thinking: A Seeker's ABC* (San Francisco: HarperOne, 1993), 118.

2. Erik H. Erikson, *The Life Cycle Completed*, extended version with new chapters on the ninth stage of development by Joan M. Erikson (New York: W. W. Norton, 1998) 50.

3. Kerrie Graham and Gordon Burghardt, "Current Perspectives on the Biological Study of Play: Signs of Progress," *The Quarterly Review of Biology* 85, no. 4 (December 2010): 393–418, doi: 10.1086/656903.

4. "A Scholarly Blog on Play," PlayCore, https://www.playcore.com/drstuartbrown.

5. Erik H. Erikson, *The Life Cycle Completed*, extended version with new chapters on the ninth stage of development by Joan M. Erikson (New York: W. W. Norton, 1998), 77.

6. Ibid.

7. Leonard Sweet, *The Well-Played Life: Why Pleasing God Doesn't Have to Be Such Hard Work* (Carol Stream, IL: Tyndale Momentum, 2014).

8. The exception, of course, is any childhood riddled with real threat, abuse, and terror. In cases in which the world is, on the whole, a life-threatening place for the child, the inverse is true.

9. Kenneth R. Ginsburg, the Committee on Communications and the Committee on Psychosocial Aspects of Child and Family Health, "The Importance of Play in Promoting Healthy Child Development and Maintaining Strong Parent-Child Bonds," *Pediatrics* 119, no. 1 (January 2007): 182–91, https://doi.org/10.1542/peds.2006-2697.

10. *Strong's Concordance*, Bible Hub, "pros," https://biblehub.com/greek/4314.htm.

11. Specifically, 1 John 3:1, but also Matthew 19:14; Galatians 3:26; 4:7; 2 Corinthians 6:18; Romans 8:14; John 1:12.

Day 2: The Student

1. I am not using adolescence as a technical term here. Technically, the term is often used in correspondence with puberty (a physical transition from child to adult). I am not using the term in that sense, but rather as a phenomenological transition that includes the physical as well as the psychological, social, and neurological changes we all undergo.

2. Research shows this can slow between ages 20–25: Vivian Giang, "What It Takes to Change Your Brain's Patterns After Age 25," *Fast Company*, April 28, 2015, https://www.fastcompany.com/3045424/what-it-takes-to-change-your-brains-patterns-after-age-25; Graham Lawton, "The Five Ages of the Brain: Adulthood," *New Scientist*, April 1, 2009, https://www.newscientist.com/article/mg20227023-000-the-five-ages-of-the-brain-adulthood; "At What Age Is the Brain Fully Developed?," Mental Health Daily, February 18, 2015, https://mentalhealth

daily.com/2015/02/18/at-what-age-is-the-brain-fully-developed; Ferris Jabr, "The Neuroscience of 20-Somethings," *Scientific American*, August 29, 2012, https://blogs.scientificamerican.com/brainwaves/the-neuroscience-of-twenty-somethings.

3. Jonathan T. Taplin, *Move Fast and Break Things: How Facebook, Google, and Amazon Cornered Culture and What It Means for All of Us* (New York: Little, Brown and Company, 2017).

4. Frances Jensen, *Teenage Brain: A Neuroscientist's Survival Guide to Raising Adolescents and Young Adults* (Toronto: HarperCollins Canada, 2015), 83.

5. Josh Shipp, *The Grown-Up's Guide to Teenage Humans: How to Decode Their Behavior, Develop Trust, and Raise a Respectable Adult* (New York: Harper Wave, an imprint of HarperCollins, 2018), 23–24.

6. Erik H. Erikson, *Childhood and Society* (New York: W. W. Norton, 1993), 8.

7. Kevin D. Mahoney and the Latdict Group, "Latin Definition for: Adolesco, Adolescere, Adolevi, Adultus," *Oxford Latin Dictionary 1982 (Old)* (Oxford: Oxford University Press, 1982), https://latin-dictionary.net/definition/1262/adolesco-adolescere-adolevi-adultus.

Day 3: The Worker

1. Erik H. Erikson, *The Life Cycle Completed*, extended version with new chapters on the ninth stage of development by Joan M. Erikson (New York: W. W. Norton, 1998).

2. Kenneth Keniston, "Youth: A 'New' Stage of Life," *The American Scholar* 39, no. 4 (1970): 631–54, http://www.jstor.org/stable/41209802.

3. Meg Jay, *The Defining Decade: Why Your Twenties Matter and How to Make the Most of Them Now* (New York: Twelve, 2012).

4. Jeffrey Jensen Arnett, *Emerging Adulthood: The Winding Road from the Late Teens through the Twenties* (New York: Oxford University Press, 2015), 17.

5. David Brooks, *The Second Mountain: The Quest for a Moral Life* (New York: Random House, 2019), ix–xx.

6. Also in Matthew 16:24; Mark 8:34; Luke 9:23; 14:27.

7. Robert M. Yerkes and John D. Dodson, "The Relation of Strength of Stimulus to Rapidity of Habit-Formation," *Journal of Comparative Neurology and Psychology* 18, no. 5 (November 1908): 459–82, https://doi.org/10.1002/cne.920180503.

8. Mihaly Csikszentmihalyi, *Flow: The Psychology of Optimal Experience* (New York: Harper & Row, 1990).

9. J. Robert Clinton, *The Making of a Leader: Recognizing the Lessons and Stages of Leadership Development* (Rapid City, SD: Two Words Publishing, LLC, 2017).

10. James E. Côté and Charles G. Levine, *Identity, Formation, Agency, and Culture: A Social Psychological Synthesis* (Oxfordshire, UK: Taylor & Francis, 2014), 141–145.

11. Malcolm Gladwell, *Outliers: The Story of Success* (New York: Hachette Audio, 2008).

12. K. Anders Ericsson, Ralf Th. Krampe, and Clemens Tesch-Römer, "The Role of Deliberate Practice in the Acquisition of Expert Performance," *Psychological Review* 100, no. 3 (1993): 363–406, https://doi.org/10.1037/0033-295x.100.3.363.

13. Krista K. Payne, "Median Age at First Marriage, 2017," Family Profiles, FP-19-06, 2019, Bowling Green, OH: National Center for Family & Marriage Research, https://doi.org/10.25035/ncfmr/fp-19-06.

14. Alexander Plateris, "Duration of marriage to divorce, United States," Vital and health statistics, Series 21, Data from the national vital statistics system, no. 38, https://www.cdc.gov/nchs/data/series/sr_21/sr21_038.pdf.

15. Sally C. Clarke, "Advance report of final divorce statistics, 1989 and 1990," Monthly vital statistics report, Vol. 43, no. 8, U.S. Department of Health and Human Services, Hyattsville, Maryland, 1995, https://www.cdc.gov/nchs/data/mvsr/supp/mv43_09s.pdf.

16. Søren Kierkegaard, Reidar Thomte, and Albert B. Anderson, *The Concept of Anxiety: A Simple Psychologically Orienting Deliberation on the Dogmatic Issue of Hereditary Sin* (Princeton, NJ: Princeton University Press, 1992).

Interlude: Transitions, the Nighttime of Decision

1. Saint John of the Cross, *The Dark Night of the Soul*, translated by David Lewis (London: T. Baker, 1908).

2. Saint Ignatius (of Loyola), *The Spiritual Exercises of St. Ignatius*, translated by Anthony Mottola (New York: Image Books, 2014), 130.

Day 4: The Maker

1. Thomas G. West, and Plato, *Plato's Apology of Socrates: an interpretation, with a new translation* (Ithaca, NY: Cornell University Press, 1979).

2. Sheldon Kopp, *Blues Ain't Nothing But a Good Soul Feeling Bad: Daily Steps to Spiritual Growth* (London: Atria Books, 2013), 9.

3. *Joseph Campbell and The Power of Myth with Bill Moyers* (documentary), PBS, 1988.

4. Michael Block, "Identity Versus Role Confusion," *Encyclopedia of Child Behavior and Development*, S. Goldstein, J.A. Naglieri (eds) (Boston: Springer, 2011), https://doi.org/10.1007/978-0-387-79061-9_1447.

5. You can learn more about the UNDERGROUND by visiting undergroundnetwork.org, reading my book *Underground Church* (Grand Rapids, MI: 2018), or watching the documentary called "Underground People."

6. To learn more about this process and the breathtaking possibilities for mission, consider reading my book *Microchurches, A Smaller Way* (Tampa, FL: Underground Media, 2019).

Interlude: The Prayer of Indifference

1. Ruth Haley Barton, "Advent 4: Mary and the Prayer of Indifference," Transforming Center, December 13, 2011, https://transformingcenter.org/2011/12/advent-4-mary-and-the-prayer-of-indifference.

Day 5: The Mentor

1. As quoted by Mel Gibson in *Braveheart* (film), Paramount Pictures, 1995.

2. Ridley Scott, 2005. *Gladiator* (film) Universal City, CA: DreamWorks Home Entertainment: Universal Studios, 2000.

3. M. Craig Barnes, *The Pastor as Minor Poet: Texts and Subtexts in the Ministerial Life* (Grand Rapids, MI: Eerdmans, 2009), 49.

4. C. L. Slater, "Generativity Versus Stagnation: An Elaboration of Erikson's Adult Stage of Human Development," *Journal of Adult Development* 10, no. 1 (2003): 53–65. https://doi.org/10.1023/A:1020790820868.

5. Barbara M. Newman and Philip R. Newman, *Development through Life: A Psychosocial Approach* (Boston: Cengage, 2014), 513.

6. Gordon MacKenzie, *Orbiting the Giant Hairball: A Corporate Fool's Guide to Surviving with Grace* (New York: Viking, 1998), 148.

7. Ibid., 149–51

Interlude: The Descent of Leadership

1. Brian Sanders, "The Descent of Leadership," Medium (blog), June 5, 2020, https://bsunderground.medium.com/the-descent-of-leadership-97012a22cee.

2. Plutarch, *Moralia*, translated by Frank Cole Babbitt (Cambridge, MA: Harvard University Press, 2000).

3. "Emeritus," Merriam-Webster Dictionary, https://www.merriam-web ster.com/dictionary/emeritus.

4. C. S. Lewis, *The Weight of Glory* (New York: HarperCollins, 2001), 37.

Day 6: The Mystic

1. Oscar A. Romero, *The Violence of Love*, translated by James R. Brock- man (Farmington, PA: The Bruderhof Foundation, Inc., 2003), 134.

2. United Nations, Department of Economic and Social Affairs, Popu- lation Division (2017). "World Mortality Report 2017," CD-ROM Edition–Datasets in Excel formats (POP/DB/MORT/2017).

3. Neil Cole, *Organic Leadership: Leading Naturally Right Where You Are* (Grand Rapids, MI: Baker Books, 2009), 156.

4. A version of this article appears in print on July 7, 2013, Section SR, Page 12 of the New York edition with the headline: "The Joy of Old Age. (No Kidding.)" https://www.nytimes.com/2013/07/07/opin ion/sunday/the-joy-of-old-age-no-kidding.html.

5. M. Scott Peck, *The Different Drum: Community Making and Peace* (New York: Touchstone, 2010), 192.

6. Frances E. Aboud and Kenneth J. Gergen, *Social Psychology in Transi- tion* (Germany: Springer US, 2012), 47.

7. A. Weiss, J. E. King, M. Inoue-Murayama, T. Matsuzawa, and A. J. Os- wald. "Evidence for a Midlife Crisis in Great Apes Consistent with the U-Shape in Human Well-Being." *Proceedings of the National Academy of Sciences* 109, no. 49 (2012), 19949–52. https://doi.org/10.1073/ pnas.1212592109.

8. Andrew Oswald and Nattavudh Powdthavee, "Happiness and Work," University of Warwick, UK, presented in Vienna, 2017, http://andrew oswald.com/docs/Vienna-talk-Happiness-at-Work-November-2017. ppt.

9. William Shakespeare, *As You Like It: A Comedy* (London: S. Gos- nell, 1810), Act II Scene VII, 34–35.

10. G. K. Chesterton, *Orthodoxy* (Wheaton, IL: Harold Shaw Publishers, 1994), 61.

11. Julianne Holt-Lunstad, "The Health Impact of Loneliness: Emerging Evidence and Interventions," NIHCM, October 15, 2018, https:// nihcm.org/publications/the-health-impact-of-loneliness-emerging -evidence-and-interventions.

12. Ronald Rolheiser, *Sacred Fire: A Vision for a Deeper Human and Christian Maturity* (New York: The Crown Publishing Group, 2017), 284.

13. Amelia Goranson, Ryan S. Ritter, Adam Waytz, and Michael I. Norton, and Kurt Gray, "Emotions Expressed by the Dying Are Unexpectedly Positive," Association for Psychological Science, June 1, 2017, https://www.psychologicalscience.org/news/releases/emotions-dying-positive.html.

14. Amelia Goranson, et al., "Dying Is Unexpectedly Positive," *Psychological Science* 28, no. 7 (2017): 988–99, https://doi.org/10.1177/0956797617701186.

15. Pope Benedict XVI, *Holy Women*, Our Sunday Visitor (Huntington, IN, 2011) n.p.

16. Liz Mineo, "Harvard Study, Almost 80 Years Old, Has Proved That Embracing Community Helps Us Live Longer, and Be Happier," *The Harvard Gazette*, April 11, 2017, https://news.harvard.edu/gazette/story/2017/04/over-nearly-80-years-harvard-study-has-been-show-ing-how-to-live-a-healthy-and-happy-life.

17. George E. Vaillant, *Triumphs of Experience: The Men of the Harvard Grant Study* (Cambridge, MA: The Belknap Press of Harvard University Press, 2012). 50

Transfiguration

1. Dylan Thomas, "Do not go gentle into that good night," Poem. In *The Poems of Dylan Thomas*, ed. John Goodby (New York: New Directions, 2003), 239.

HOW CAN YOU TELL IF YOU'RE ACTUALLY GROWING?

MOODY Publishers®

From the Word to Life®

Nancy Kane explores the five stages of the soul's journey toward loving God. From stage one, first love, to stage five, intimate love, you will learn where you are, how to grow in love toward God and others, and how to embrace a faith that heals and fills you.

978-0-8024-1999-6 | also available as eBook and audiobook

"I am looking for the fellowship of the burning heart—for men and women of all generations who love the Savior until adoration becomes the music of their soul."

—A. W. Tozer

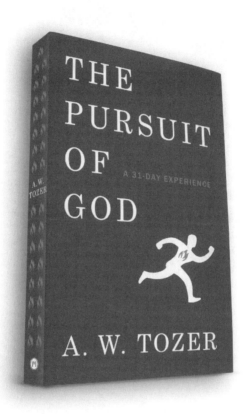

WHAT DOES ART HAVE TO DO WITH FAITH?

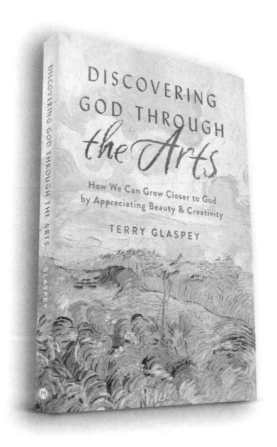

In *Discovering God through the Arts*, you'll learn how artistic works can lead to faith-building, life-changing spiritual formation for every Christian. Since art is a reflection, examination, or contemplation of the human experience, you can enrich your faith by infusing art into your spiritual journey.

978-0-8024-1997-2 I also available as an eBook